GACE

Behavioral Science
Part 1 of 2

SECRETS

Study Guide
Your Key to Exam Success

GACE Test Review for the
Georgia Assessments for the
Certification of Educators

Dear Future Exam Success Story:

First of all, **THANK YOU** for purchasing Mometrix study materials!

Second, congratulations! You are one of the few determined test-takers who are committed to doing whatever it takes to excel on your exam. **You have come to the right place.** We developed these study materials with one goal in mind: to deliver you the information you need in a format that's concise and easy to use.

In addition to optimizing your guide for the content of the test, we've outlined our recommended steps for breaking down the preparation process into small, attainable goals so you can make sure you stay on track.

We've also analyzed the entire test-taking process, identifying the most common pitfalls and showing how you can overcome them and be ready for any curveball the test throws you.

Standardized testing is one of the biggest obstacles on your road to success, which only increases the importance of doing well in the high-pressure, high-stakes environment of test day. Your results on this test could have a significant impact on your future, and this guide provides the information and practical advice to help you achieve your full potential on test day.

Your success is our success

We would love to hear from you! If you would like to share the story of your exam success or if you have any questions or comments in regard to our products, please contact us at **800-673-8175** or **support@mometrix.com**.

Thanks again for your business and we wish you continued success!

Sincerely,
The Mometrix Test Preparation Team

Need more help? Check out our flashcards at: http://MometrixFlashcards.com/GACE

TABLE OF CONTENTS

Introduction

Thank you for purchasing this resource! You have made the choice to prepare yourself for a test that could have a huge impact on your future, and this guide is designed to help you be fully ready for test day. Obviously, it's important to have a solid understanding of the test material, but you also need to be prepared for the unique environment and stressors of the test, so that you can perform to the best of your abilities.

For this purpose, the first section that appears in this guide is the **Secret Keys**. We've devoted countless hours to meticulously researching what works and what doesn't, and we've boiled down our findings to the five most impactful steps you can take to improve your performance on the test. We start at the beginning with study planning and move through the preparation process, all the way to the testing strategies that will help you get the most out of what you know when you're finally sitting in front of the test.

We recommend that you start preparing for your test as far in advance as possible. However, if you've bought this guide as a last-minute study resource and only have a few days before your test, we recommend that you skip over the first two Secret Keys since they address a long-term study plan.

If you struggle with **test anxiety**, we strongly encourage you to check out our recommendations for how you can overcome it. Test anxiety is a formidable foe, but it can be beaten, and we want to make sure you have the tools you need to defeat it.

Secret Key #1 – Plan Big, Study Small

There's a lot riding on your performance. If you want to ace this test, you're going to need to keep your skills sharp and the material fresh in your mind. You need a plan that lets you review everything you need to know while still fitting in your schedule. We'll break this strategy down into three categories.

Information Organization

Start with the information you already have: the official test outline. From this, you can make a complete list of all the concepts you need to cover before the test. Organize these concepts into groups that can be studied together, and create a list of any related vocabulary you need to learn so you can brush up on any difficult terms. You'll want to keep this vocabulary list handy once you actually start studying since you may need to add to it along the way.

Time Management

Once you have your set of study concepts, decide how to spread them out over the time you have left before the test. Break your study plan into small, clear goals so you have a manageable task for each day and know exactly what you're doing. Then just focus on one small step at a time. When you manage your time this way, you don't need to spend hours at a time studying. Studying a small block of content for a short period each day helps you retain information better and avoid stressing over how much you have left to do. You can relax knowing that you have a plan to cover everything in time. In order for this strategy to be effective though, you have to start studying early and stick to your schedule. Avoid the exhaustion and futility that comes from last-minute cramming!

Study Environment

The environment you study in has a big impact on your learning. Studying in a coffee shop, while probably more enjoyable, is not likely to be as fruitful as studying in a quiet room. It's important to keep distractions to a minimum. You're only planning to study for a short block of time, so make the most of it. Don't pause to check your phone or get up to find a snack. It's also important to **avoid multitasking**. Research has consistently shown that multitasking will make your studying dramatically less effective. Your study area should also be comfortable and well-lit so you don't have the distraction of straining your eyes or sitting on an uncomfortable chair.

The time of day you study is also important. You want to be rested and alert. Don't wait until just before bedtime. Study when you'll be most likely to comprehend and remember. Even better, if you know what time of day your test will be, set that time aside for study. That way your brain will be used to working on that subject at that specific time and you'll have a better chance of recalling information.

Finally, it can be helpful to team up with others who are studying for the same test. Your actual studying should be done in as isolated an environment as possible, but the work of organizing the information and setting up the study plan can be divided up. In between study sessions, you can discuss with your teammates the concepts that you're all studying and quiz each other on the details. Just be sure that your teammates are as serious about the test as you are. If you find that your study time is being replaced with social time, you might need to find a new team.

Secret Key #2 – Make Your Studying Count

You're devoting a lot of time and effort to preparing for this test, so you want to be absolutely certain it will pay off. This means doing more than just reading the content and hoping you can remember it on test day. It's important to make every minute of study count. There are two main areas you can focus on to make your studying count:

Retention

It doesn't matter how much time you study if you can't remember the material. You need to make sure you are retaining the concepts. To check your retention of the information you're learning, try recalling it at later times with minimal prompting. Try carrying around flashcards and glance at one or two from time to time or ask a friend who's also studying for the test to quiz you.

To enhance your retention, look for ways to put the information into practice so that you can apply it rather than simply recalling it. If you're using the information in practical ways, it will be much easier to remember. Similarly, it helps to solidify a concept in your mind if you're not only reading it to yourself but also explaining it to someone else. Ask a friend to let you teach them about a concept you're a little shaky on (or speak aloud to an imaginary audience if necessary). As you try to summarize, define, give examples, and answer your friend's questions, you'll understand the concepts better and they will stay with you longer. Finally, step back for a big picture view and ask yourself how each piece of information fits with the whole subject. When you link the different concepts together and see them working together as a whole, it's easier to remember the individual components.

Finally, practice showing your work on any multi-step problems, even if you're just studying. Writing out each step you take to solve a problem will help solidify the process in your mind, and you'll be more likely to remember it during the test.

Modality

Modality simply refers to the means or method by which you study. Choosing a study modality that fits your own individual learning style is crucial. No two people learn best in exactly the same way, so it's important to know your strengths and use them to your advantage.

For example, if you learn best by visualization, focus on visualizing a concept in your mind and draw an image or a diagram. Try color-coding your notes, illustrating them, or creating symbols that will trigger your mind to recall a learned concept. If you learn best by hearing or discussing information, find a study partner who learns the same way or read aloud to yourself. Think about how to put the information in your own words. Imagine that you are giving a lecture on the topic and record yourself so you can listen to it later.

For any learning style, flashcards can be helpful. Organize the information so you can take advantage of spare moments to review. Underline key words or phrases. Use different colors for different categories. Mnemonic devices (such as creating a short list in which every item starts with the same letter) can also help with retention. Find what works best for you and use it to store the information in your mind most effectively and easily.

Secret Key #3 – Practice the Right Way

Your success on test day depends not only on how many hours you put into preparing, but also on whether you prepared the right way. It's good to check along the way to see if your studying is paying off. One of the most effective ways to do this is by taking practice tests to evaluate your progress. Practice tests are useful because they show exactly where you need to improve. Every time you take a practice test, pay special attention to these three groups of questions:

- The questions you got wrong
- The questions you had to guess on, even if you guessed right
- The questions you found difficult or slow to work through

This will show you exactly what your weak areas are, and where you need to devote more study time. Ask yourself why each of these questions gave you trouble. Was it because you didn't understand the material? Was it because you didn't remember the vocabulary? Do you need more repetitions on this type of question to build speed and confidence? Dig into those questions and figure out how you can strengthen your weak areas as you go back to review the material.

Additionally, many practice tests have a section explaining the answer choices. It can be tempting to read the explanation and think that you now have a good understanding of the concept. However, an explanation likely only covers part of the question's broader context. Even if the explanation makes sense, **go back and investigate** every concept related to the question until you're positive you have a thorough understanding.

As you go along, keep in mind that the practice test is just that: practice. Memorizing these questions and answers will not be very helpful on the actual test because it is unlikely to have any of the same exact questions. If you only know the right answers to the sample questions, you won't be prepared for the real thing. **Study the concepts** until you understand them fully, and then you'll be able to answer any question that shows up on the test.

It's important to wait on the practice tests until you're ready. If you take a test on your first day of study, you may be overwhelmed by the amount of material covered and how much you need to learn. Work up to it gradually.

On test day, you'll need to be prepared for answering questions, managing your time, and using the test-taking strategies you've learned. It's a lot to balance, like a mental marathon that will have a big impact on your future. Like training for a marathon, you'll need to start slowly and work your way up. When test day arrives, you'll be ready.

Start with the strategies you've read in the first two Secret Keys—plan your course and study in the way that works best for you. If you have time, consider using multiple study resources to get different approaches to the same concepts. It can be helpful to see difficult concepts from more than one angle. Then find a good source for practice tests. Many times, the test website will suggest potential study resources or provide sample tests.

Practice Test Strategy

When you're ready to start taking practice tests, follow this strategy:

Untimed and Open-Book Practice

Take the first test with no time constraints and with your notes and study guide handy. Take your time and focus on applying the strategies you've learned.

Timed and Open-Book Practice

Take the second practice test open-book as well, but set a timer and practice pacing yourself to finish in time.

Timed and Closed-Book Practice

Take any other practice tests as if it were test day. Set a timer and put away your study materials. Sit at a table or desk in a quiet room, imagine yourself at the testing center, and answer questions as quickly and accurately as possible.

Keep repeating timed and closed-book tests on a regular basis until you run out of practice tests or it's time for the actual test. Your mind will be ready for the schedule and stress of test day, and you'll be able to focus on recalling the material you've learned.

Secret Key #4 – Pace Yourself

Once you're fully prepared for the material on the test, your biggest challenge on test day will be managing your time. Just knowing that the clock is ticking can make you panic even if you have plenty of time left. Work on pacing yourself so you can build confidence against the time constraints of the exam. Pacing is a difficult skill to master, especially in a high-pressure environment, so **practice is vital**.

Set time expectations for your pace based on how much time is available. For example, if a section has 60 questions and the time limit is 30 minutes, you know you have to average 30 seconds or less per question in order to answer them all. Although 30 seconds is the hard limit, set 25 seconds per question as your goal, so you reserve extra time to spend on harder questions. When you budget extra time for the harder questions, you no longer have any reason to stress when those questions take longer to answer.

Don't let this time expectation distract you from working through the test at a calm, steady pace, but keep it in mind so you don't spend too much time on any one question. Recognize that taking extra time on one question you don't understand may keep you from answering two that you do understand later in the test. If your time limit for a question is up and you're still not sure of the answer, mark it and move on, and come back to it later if the time and the test format allow. If the testing format doesn't allow you to return to earlier questions, just make an educated guess; then put it out of your mind and move on.

On the easier questions, be careful not to rush. It may seem wise to hurry through them so you have more time for the challenging ones, but it's not worth missing one if you know the concept and just didn't take the time to read the question fully. Work efficiently but make sure you understand the question and have looked at all of the answer choices, since more than one may seem right at first.

Even if you're paying attention to the time, you may find yourself a little behind at some point. You should speed up to get back on track, but do so wisely. Don't panic; just take a few seconds less on each question until you're caught up. Don't guess without thinking, but do look through the answer choices and eliminate any you know are wrong. If you can get down to two choices, it is often worthwhile to guess from those. Once you've chosen an answer, move on and don't dwell on any that you skipped or had to hurry through. If a question was taking too long, chances are it was one of the harder ones, so you weren't as likely to get it right anyway.

On the other hand, if you find yourself getting ahead of schedule, it may be beneficial to slow down a little. The more quickly you work, the more likely you are to make a careless mistake that will affect your score. You've budgeted time for each question, so don't be afraid to spend that time. Practice an efficient but careful pace to get the most out of the time you have.

Secret Key #5 – Have a Plan for Guessing

When you're taking the test, you may find yourself stuck on a question. Some of the answer choices seem better than others, but you don't see the one answer choice that is obviously correct. What do you do?

The scenario described above is very common, yet most test takers have not effectively prepared for it. Developing and practicing a plan for guessing may be one of the single most effective uses of your time as you get ready for the exam.

In developing your plan for guessing, there are three questions to address:

- When should you start the guessing process?
- How should you narrow down the choices?
- Which answer should you choose?

When to Start the Guessing Process

Unless your plan for guessing is to select C every time (which, despite its merits, is not what we recommend), you need to leave yourself enough time to apply your answer elimination strategies. Since you have a limited amount of time for each question, that means that if you're going to give yourself the best shot at guessing correctly, you have to decide quickly whether or not you will guess.

Of course, the best-case scenario is that you don't have to guess at all, so first, see if you can answer the question based on your knowledge of the subject and basic reasoning skills. Focus on the key words in the question and try to jog your memory of related topics. Give yourself a chance to bring the knowledge to mind, but once you realize that you don't have (or you can't access) the knowledge you need to answer the question, it's time to start the guessing process.

It's almost always better to start the guessing process too early than too late. It only takes a few seconds to remember something and answer the question from knowledge. Carefully eliminating wrong answer choices takes longer. Plus, going through the process of eliminating answer choices can actually help jog your memory.

Summary: Start the guessing process as soon as you decide that you can't answer the question based on your knowledge.

How to Narrow Down the Choices

The next chapter in this book (**Test-Taking Strategies**) includes a wide range of strategies for how to approach questions and how to look for answer choices to eliminate. You will definitely want to read those carefully, practice them, and figure out which ones work best for you. Here though, we're going to address a mindset rather than a particular strategy.

Your chances of guessing an answer correctly depend on how many options you are choosing from.

How many choices you have	How likely you are to guess correctly
5	20%
4	25%
3	33%
2	50%
1	100%

You can see from this chart just how valuable it is to be able to eliminate incorrect answers and make an educated guess, but there are two things that many test takers do that cause them to miss out on the benefits of guessing:

- Accidentally eliminating the correct answer
- Selecting an answer based on an impression

We'll look at the first one here, and the second one in the next section.

To avoid accidentally eliminating the correct answer, we recommend a thought exercise called **the $5 challenge**. In this challenge, you only eliminate an answer choice from contention if you are willing to bet $5 on it being wrong. Why $5? Five dollars is a small but not insignificant amount of money. It's an amount you could afford to lose but wouldn't want to throw away. And while losing $5 once might not hurt too much, doing it twenty times will set you back $100. In the same way, each small decision you make—eliminating a choice here, guessing on a question there—won't by itself impact your score very much, but when you put them all together, they can make a big difference. By holding each answer choice elimination decision to a higher standard, you can reduce the risk of accidentally eliminating the correct answer.

The $5 challenge can also be applied in a positive sense: If you are willing to bet $5 that an answer choice *is* correct, go ahead and mark it as correct.

Summary: Only eliminate an answer choice if you are willing to bet $5 that it is wrong.

Which Answer to Choose

You're taking the test. You've run into a hard question and decided you'll have to guess. You've eliminated all the answer choices you're willing to bet $5 on. Now you have to pick an answer. Why do we even need to talk about this? Why can't you just pick whichever one you feel like when the time comes?

The answer to these questions is that if you don't come into the test with a plan, you'll rely on your impression to select an answer choice, and if you do that, you risk falling into a trap. The test writers know that everyone who takes their test will be guessing on some of the questions, so they intentionally write wrong answer choices to seem plausible. You still have to pick an answer though, and if the wrong answer choices are designed to look right, how can you ever be sure that you're not falling for their trap? The best solution we've found to this dilemma is to take the decision out of your hands entirely. Here is the process we recommend:

Once you've eliminated any choices that you are confident (willing to bet $5) are wrong, select the first remaining choice as your answer.

Whether you choose to select the first remaining choice, the second, or the last, the important thing is that you use some preselected standard. Using this approach guarantees that you will not be enticed into selecting an answer choice that looks right, because you are not basing your decision on how the answer choices look.

This is not meant to make you question your knowledge. Instead, it is to help you recognize the difference between your knowledge and your impressions. There's a huge difference between thinking an answer is right because of what you know, and thinking an answer is right because it looks or sounds like it should be right.

Summary: To ensure that your selection is appropriately random, make a predetermined selection from among all answer choices you have not eliminated.

Test-Taking Strategies

This section contains a list of test-taking strategies that you may find helpful as you work through the test. By taking what you know and applying logical thought, you can maximize your chances of answering any question correctly!

It is very important to realize that every question is different and every person is different: no single strategy will work on every question, and no single strategy will work for every person. That's why we've included all of them here, so you can try them out and determine which ones work best for different types of questions and which ones work best for you.

Question Strategies

Read Carefully

Read the question and answer choices carefully. Don't miss the question because you misread the terms. You have plenty of time to read each question thoroughly and make sure you understand what is being asked. Yet a happy medium must be attained, so don't waste too much time. You must read carefully, but efficiently.

Contextual Clues

Look for contextual clues. If the question includes a word you are not familiar with, look at the immediate context for some indication of what the word might mean. Contextual clues can often give you all the information you need to decipher the meaning of an unfamiliar word. Even if you can't determine the meaning, you may be able to narrow down the possibilities enough to make a solid guess at the answer to the question.

Prefixes

If you're having trouble with a word in the question or answer choices, try dissecting it. Take advantage of every clue that the word might include. Prefixes and suffixes can be a huge help. Usually they allow you to determine a basic meaning. Pre- means before, post- means after, pro - is positive, de- is negative. From prefixes and suffixes, you can get an idea of the general meaning of the word and try to put it into context.

Hedge Words

Watch out for critical hedge words, such as *likely, may, can, sometimes, often, almost, mostly, usually, generally, rarely*, and *sometimes*. Question writers insert these hedge phrases to cover every possibility. Often an answer choice will be wrong simply because it leaves no room for exception. Be on guard for answer choices that have definitive words such as *exactly* and *always*.

Switchback Words

Stay alert for *switchbacks*. These are the words and phrases frequently used to alert you to shifts in thought. The most common switchback words are *but, although*, and *however*. Others include *nevertheless, on the other hand, even though, while, in spite of, despite, regardless of*. Switchback words are important to catch because they can change the direction of the question or an answer choice.

- 10 -

Face Value

When in doubt, use common sense. Accept the situation in the problem at face value. Don't read too much into it. These problems will not require you to make wild assumptions. If you have to go beyond creativity and warp time or space in order to have an answer choice fit the question, then you should move on and consider the other answer choices. These are normal problems rooted in reality. The applicable relationship or explanation may not be readily apparent, but it is there for you to figure out. Use your common sense to interpret anything that isn't clear.

Answer Choice Strategies

Answer Selection

The most thorough way to pick an answer choice is to identify and eliminate wrong answers until only one is left, then confirm it is the correct answer. Sometimes an answer choice may immediately seem right, but be careful. The test writers will usually put more than one reasonable answer choice on each question, so take a second to read all of them and make sure that the other choices are not equally obvious. As long as you have time left, it is better to read every answer choice than to pick the first one that looks right without checking the others.

Answer Choice Families

An answer choice family consists of two (in rare cases, three) answer choices that are very similar in construction and cannot all be true at the same time. If you see two answer choices that are direct opposites or parallels, one of them is usually the correct answer. For instance, if one answer choice says that quantity x increases and another either says that quantity x decreases (opposite) or says that quantity y increases (parallel), then those answer choices would fall into the same family. An answer choice that doesn't match the construction of the answer choice family is more likely to be incorrect. Most questions will not have answer choice families, but when they do appear, you should be prepared to recognize them.

Eliminate Answers

Eliminate answer choices as soon as you realize they are wrong, but make sure you consider all possibilities. If you are eliminating answer choices and realize that the last one you are left with is also wrong, don't panic. Start over and consider each choice again. There may be something you missed the first time that you will realize on the second pass.

Avoid Fact Traps

Don't be distracted by an answer choice that is factually true but doesn't answer the question. You are looking for the choice that answers the question. Stay focused on what the question is asking for so you don't accidentally pick an answer that is true but incorrect. Always go back to the question and make sure the answer choice you've selected actually answers the question and is not merely a true statement.

Extreme Statements

In general, you should avoid answers that put forth extreme actions as standard practice or proclaim controversial ideas as established fact. An answer choice that states the "process should be used in certain situations, if…" is much more likely to be correct than one that states the "process should be discontinued completely." The first is a calm rational statement and doesn't even make a definitive, uncompromising stance, using a hedge word *if* to provide wiggle room, whereas the second choice is a radical idea and far more extreme.

Benchmark

As you read through the answer choices and you come across one that seems to answer the question well, mentally select that answer choice. This is not your final answer, but it's the one that will help you evaluate the other answer choices. The one that you selected is your benchmark or standard for judging each of the other answer choices. Every other answer choice must be compared to your benchmark. That choice is correct until proven otherwise by another answer choice beating it. If you find a better answer, then that one becomes your new benchmark. Once you've decided that no other choice answers the question as well as your benchmark, you have your final answer.

Predict the Answer

Before you even start looking at the answer choices, it is often best to try to predict the answer. When you come up with the answer on your own, it is easier to avoid distractions and traps because you will know exactly what to look for. The right answer choice is unlikely to be word-for-word what you came up with, but it should be a close match. Even if you are confident that you have the right answer, you should still take the time to read each option before moving on.

General Strategies

Tough Questions

If you are stumped on a problem or it appears too hard or too difficult, don't waste time. Move on! Remember though, if you can quickly check for obviously incorrect answer choices, your chances of guessing correctly are greatly improved. Before you completely give up, at least try to knock out a couple of possible answers. Eliminate what you can and then guess at the remaining answer choices before moving on.

Check Your Work

Since you will probably not know every term listed and the answer to every question, it is important that you get credit for the ones that you do know. Don't miss any questions through careless mistakes. If at all possible, try to take a second to look back over your answer selection and make sure you've selected the correct answer choice and haven't made a costly careless mistake (such as marking an answer choice that you didn't mean to mark). This quick double check should more than pay for itself in caught mistakes for the time it costs.

Pace Yourself

It's easy to be overwhelmed when you're looking at a page full of questions; your mind is confused and full of random thoughts, and the clock is ticking down faster than you would like. Calm down and maintain the pace that you have set for yourself. Especially as you get down to the last few minutes of the test, don't let the small numbers on the clock make you panic. As long as you are on track by monitoring your pace, you are guaranteed to have time for each question.

Don't Rush

It is very easy to make errors when you are in a hurry. Maintaining a fast pace in answering questions is pointless if it makes you miss questions that you would have gotten right otherwise. Test writers like to include distracting information and wrong answers that seem right. Taking a little extra time to avoid careless mistakes can make all the difference in your test score. Find a pace that allows you to be confident in the answers that you select.

Keep Moving

Panicking will not help you pass the test, so do your best to stay calm and keep moving. Taking deep breaths and going through the answer elimination steps you practiced can help to break through a stress barrier and keep your pace.

Final Notes

The combination of a solid foundation of content knowledge and the confidence that comes from practicing your plan for applying that knowledge is the key to maximizing your performance on test day. As your foundation of content knowledge is built up and strengthened, you'll find that the strategies included in this chapter become more and more effective in helping you quickly sift through the distractions and traps of the test to isolate the correct answer.

Now it's time to move on to the test content chapters of this book, but be sure to keep your goal in mind. As you read, think about how you will be able to apply this information on the test. If you've already seen sample questions for the test and you have an idea of the question format and style, try to come up with questions of your own that you can answer based on what you're reading. This will give you valuable practice applying your knowledge in the same ways you can expect to on test day.

Good luck and good studying!

Psychology

The Empirical Approach and the Scientific Method

Empirical science requires that one gains knowledge through experience (i.e., the senses), as opposed to rationalism, which asserts that one gains knowledge through logic and reason. The empirical approach (gaining knowledge through experience) led to scientific enquiry, in which facts and evidence are gathered through observation and experiments.

The definition of the scientific method in the *Oxford English Dictionary* states that it is "a method or procedure that has characterized natural science since the 17th century, consisting of systematic observation, measurement, and experiment and the formulation, testing, and modification of hypotheses." In essence, the scientific method is a process of developing and testing theories. Said theories may be formed in the process of conceptualizing problems. A hypothesis is a testable prediction that one arrives at logically from a theory. Psychological studies follow the scientific method, including experiments, case studies, and surveys. The scientific method requires critical thinking. Without critical thinking, one cannot utilize logic to make conclusions.

Theory and Hypothesis

A theory is a proposed explanation of a phenomenon or behavior that is typically based on observation or previous research. Theories are often not proven and through further research may be modified or completely rejected. A hypothesis is typically a one-sentence statement that aims to predict the certain phenomenon to be tested in the research experiment. Based on the results of the research, the hypothesis is either supported or not supported. Both theories and hypotheses are components that are tested or further explored for scientific research. Both components are essential in an experiment because they provide support for the purpose of the study as well as the focus of what the researcher hopes to or expects to find with the results.

Behavioral Psychology

The basis of behavioral psychology is that all behaviors are learned. This school of psychology, founded by John B. Watson, is based on the belief that behaviors can be measured, trained, and changed. This perspective became dominant in the early half of the 20th century due to the work of B. F. Skinner and John B. Watson. Watson's paper, "Psychology as the Behaviorist Views It," established the school of behavioral psychology in 1913. Behavioral psychology theorizes that all behaviors are acquired through conditioning, which occurs through interaction with one's environment.

Behaviorism asserts that one can study behavior in a systematic and observable manner and need not consider internal mental states. Behaviorism studies only observable behaviors and sees internal states, such as cognitions, emotions, and moods, as too subjective. The strict behaviorist would believe that any individual could potentially be trained to perform any task without regard to genetic background, personality, or internal processes as long as he or she experiences the right conditioning.

Critics of behaviorism assert that this approach is a one-dimensional way of understanding human behavior and that behavioral theories do not account for types of learning that occur without the use of reinforcement and punishment. They also do not account for the idea of free will and other internal influences like moods, thoughts, and feelings.

Behavioral psychology has brought us useful approaches to changing maladaptive or harmful behaviors through intensive behavioral intervention, behavior analysis, and token economies. Behaviorism is easier to quantify and collect data and information than some other schools of psychology when one is conducting research.

Cognitive Psychology

Cognitive psychology studies the mind, mental function, mental processes that affect behavior including learning, memory, attention, perception, reasoning, language, conceptual development, and decision-making. The work of cognitive psychology is present in other psychological disciplines, including social psychology, educational psychology, psychology of personality, abnormal psychology, and developmental psychology.

Humanistic Psychology

Humanistic psychology has five basic principles, which are as follows:

- Human beings cannot be reduced to components and, as human, surpass the sum of their parts.
- The existence of human beings is within both a uniquely human context and a cosmic ecology.
- Human beings are conscious; that is, they are both aware and aware of their awareness. This includes an awareness of self in relation to others.
- Human beings have choice and responsibility.
- Human beings seek creativity, meaning, and value. They seek goals, act with intention, and have awareness of their roles in future events.

The perspective of humanistic psychology rose in response to what adherents see as the limitations of the work of Sigmund Freud and his psychoanalytic theory and the behaviorism of B. F. Skinner. This approach emphasizes the natural drive of the individual toward self-actualization and creativity. It focuses on creativity, free will, and human potential and asserts that people are inherently good. An early source of humanistic psychology comes from the work of Carl Rogers, who in turn was deeply influenced by the work of Otto Rank (who broke away from Freud in the mid-1920s). Rogers coined the phrase "actualizing tendency," and this concept later led Abraham Maslow to study the topic of self-actualization as one of the needs that humans have. Maslow and Rogers worked in response to what they viewed as the overly pessimistic view of psychoanalysis. They introduced a more positive response in humanistic psychology, which some see more as a perspective on the human condition that informs psychological research and practice than as a discipline within psychology. One later development in psychology that would not have occurred without humanistic psychology is the idea of emotional intelligence.

Behaviorist Versus Humanistic Psychology

Behaviorist psychology focuses on the mind by observing human behaviors. This school of thought asserts that whereas one cannot measure or observe feelings, human actions can reveal emotions. Humanistic psychology focuses on the current environment of the individual in determining the reasons for behaviors. Humanistic psychology does not see looking into the past (as with psychoanalysis) as sufficient to obtain a clear picture of the individual. Both these fields of psychology focus on observing human actions; however, behavioral psychology focuses on objective observations with no consideration for internal mental processes of the individuals,

- 16 -

whereas humanistic psychology focuses on the individual's potential for growth by determining what in their environment needs to be changed to improve functioning.

Biological Psychology

The biological approach to psychology is also known as behavioral neuroscience, psychobiology, or biopsychology. It applies the principles of biology, specifically neurobiology, to the study of developmental, physiological, and genetic mechanisms of behavior in both humans and nonhuman animals. This approach studies at the level of basic biological processes, neurons, neurotransmitters, and brain circuitry that lie beneath behavior, both normal and abnormal. Many experiments in this area of psychology involve animal (nonhuman) subjects such as rats, mice, and nonhuman primates but enhance the understanding of human pathology.

Principles of Biological Psychology

William James wrote *The Principles of Psychobiology* in 1890, and in it he asserts that psychology as a scientific study should be based on an understanding of biology. Many early psychologists, including James, had significant training in physiology. Biological psychologists explore similar themes as other psychologists but are limited by the need to use nonhuman animals. Because of this, much of the literature in this area of psychology explores mental processes and behaviors that are shared across species, including the following:

- Emotion
- Biological rhythms and sleep
- Memory and learning
- Movement control
- Motivated behavior (i.e., sex, hunger, thirst)
- Perception and sensation

Recent technological advances and the increasing sophistication of research methods allow biological psychologists to expand into other, classical, areas of psychology, including language, decision-making and reasoning, and consciousness. Biological psychology has a strong history of contributing to our understanding of medical disorders such as Parkinson's disease, Huntington's disease, Alzheimer's disease, clinical depression, schizophrenia, autism, anxiety, and substance abuse.

The Psychodynamic Approach

The psychodynamic approach, also referred to as dynamic psychology, studies the psychological forces that influence human behaviors and emotions. It explores the relationship between conscious and unconscious motivation. Psychodynamics studies the interrelationships of the mind, personality, and psyche as related to forces (mental, emotional, and motivational), particularly at the unconscious level. The psychodynamic approach can also refer to the psychoanalytical approach that Sigmund Freud and his followers developed, as inspired by the scientific theory of thermodynamics. Freud asserted that psychological energy was constant, with emotional changes consisting only of energy displacements.

Classical Freudian psychoanalysis tends to consist of treatment three to five times per week. In contrast, psychodynamic therapy can be less intensive and consist of only one to two sessions per week. Both of these types of therapy rely on a theory of inner, subconscious conflict and in which repressed feelings and behaviors rise to the patient's consciousness.

- 17 -

Psychodynamics studies changes in psychic energy among the id, ego, and superego, which are all aspects of one's personality. Freud asserted that the ego is at the heart of all psychological processes, and he sees the ego as contending with the id, the super-ego, and the world outside the self. The id is the unconscious reserve of psychic energy fueling instincts and psychic processes, otherwise known as the libido. The superego is the reservoir of an individual's morality and values and consists of both the internalization of society's most basic rules and norms (conscience) as well as the internalization of the individual's own goals (ego ideal). The ego operates as the administrator of personality and makes decisions about the pleasures that the id demands, keeping the individual safe, and the morality of the superego that it will follow.

Freud's model concentrates on the ever-changing interactions among id, ego, and superego and tries to explain human behavior in terms of these intrinsic forces or processes.

The Evolutionary Approach

The theoretical approach of evolutionary psychology endeavors to explain certain traits, both mental and psychological (including memory, language, or perception), as adaptations. In other words, evolutionary psychology views these traits as practical outcomes of the process of natural selection. A primary assertion of this approach is that the brain (also, mind) evolved to solve problems that humanity's ancient ancestors faced. In other words, this approach focuses on how evolution forms mind and behavior, primarily in humans but also in other organisms with a nervous system.

Certain behavior most likely developed as an adaptive process. In other words, individuals who adapt certain behaviors can be more likely to survive and reproduce or even to have the opportunity to reproduce (i.e., by appearing more attractive to potential mates). Evolutionary psychology can sometimes explain behaviors that may appear to make little sense (physical response to mental stress) or even those that are dysfunctional (mental illness).

Biopsychology

The biological aspects of behavior and mental processes are the focus of this subfield. Specialties within the subfield include *physiological psychology,* which studies the neural, cellular, and genetic mechanisms that cause specific behaviors by using animal models. Also included is *cognitive neuroscience,* which uses neural imaging tools to investigate the neural parallels of psychological processes in humans, and *neuropsychology,* which determines specific aspects and the extent of cognitive deficits caused by brain damage or disease through the use of psychological assessments.

Clinical and Cognitive Psychology

Clinical psychology studies and applies psychology to understand, prevent, and treat psychologically based dysfunction. Many clinical psychologists concentrate on psychological assessments and psychotherapy, and many primarily seek to promote well-being and personal development. Some clinical psychologists engage in other areas of practice, such as research, teaching, consultation, or forensic testimony. Within clinical psychology there are four primary theoretical approaches. These are psychodynamic, cognitive behavioral, existential-humanistic, and systems therapy approaches.

The subfield of cognitive psychology gives its attention to the mental processes that bring about mental activity. These mental processes include perception, attention, reasoning, problem-solving, memory, learning, language, and emotion. Within cognitive psychology we can find cognitive psychologists and neuroscientists, linguists, researchers in artificial intelligence and human-computer interaction, computational neuroscientists, logicians, and cognitive social psychologists.

Developmental and Learning Psychology

Developmental psychologists endeavor to understand the processes of the development of the human mind throughout the life span. This subfield of psychology examines how people perceive, understand, and behave within the world and how all of these change as they grow older. Developmental psychologists are particularly interested in cognitive, affective/emotional, moral, social, and neural development. Research in this area tends to focus on the ages that experience rapid change, such as infancy, adolescence, and older adulthood.

Learning psychology, more commonly referred to as educational psychology, is the subfield of psychology that deals with the scientific study of learning in human beings. Psychologists in this subfield examine individual difference in intelligence, cognitive development, affect, motivation, self-regulation, and self-concept and how all of these play roles in learning. Educational psychology is interested in the study of memory, conceptual processes, and individual differences in coming up with new strategies for learning processes in human beings. Theories that influence learning psychology are operant conditioning, functionalism, structuralism, constructivism, humanistic psychology, Gestalt psychology, and information processing.

Industrial-Organizational Psychology

Industrial-organizational (I-O) psychologists apply psychological concepts and techniques to improve human potential in the workplace. One area of I-O psychology, personnel psychology, seeks to utilize psychological methodology and principles to select and evaluate workers. Another subset of I-O psychology is organizational psychology, in which work environment and management styles are examined for their effect on worker motivation, job satisfaction, and productivity.

Subfields of Psychology

Personality Psychology

The subfield of personality psychology deals with long-lasting patterns of behavior, thought, and emotion in individual human beings. Different approaches to theories of personality include neo-Freudianism, trait theory, and social cognitive theory.

Sensation and Perception Psychology

The subfield of sensation and perception examines how elemental stimuli in the environment are translated into a complex psychological phenomenon, such as how light is translated into the human perception of color. All five senses are examined in this subfield as well as physiology of the sensory systems and theories of perception.

Social Psychology

The subfield of social psychology studies how human beings regard each other and how they relate to one another. This area of study deals with subjects like social influence, attitudes, prejudice, group dynamics, and social justice. Subtypes of social psychology include social cognition and social neuroscience. Social psychology is seen by many as a bridge between psychology and sociology.

Contributions of Wilhelm Wundt

Wilhelm Wundt is often called the father of psychology. He opened the first laboratory dedicated to psychology; its opening is thought of as the beginning of modern psychology. Wundt separated psychology from philosophy and studied the working of the mind in a more structured way than was previously done. In his studies he emphasized objective measurement and control. Wundt's background in physiology is evident in the topics he studied, such as the study of reaction times and sensory processes. Wundt founded the school of voluntarism, which is the process of organizing the mind. A follower of Wundt's later developed his theories and described the system as structuralism, which is the analysis of the basic elements that constitute the mind.

Wundt believed that the structure of the human mind and conscious mental states could be scientifically studied using introspection, which was a highly practiced form of self-examination. He developed a theory of conscious thought by training his psychology students to make observations that were biased by personal interpretation or previous experience. Although introspection was a great focus of Wundt's, it did not remain an elemental tool of psychological study past the early 1920s. Rather, Wundt's greatest contribution was showing that psychology could be a valid experimental science, which he did in part by conducting his research in carefully controlled conditions.

The three areas of mental functioning on which Wundt concentrated were thoughts, images, and feelings, which are the basic areas studied today in cognitive psychology. The study of perceptual processes is traced back to him, and he can be called the founder of experimental psychology.

Contributions of William James

William James has been called the "father of American psychology." He is best known for his association with the philosophical school of pragmatism, as a founder of functional psychology, as well as the James Lange theory of emotion. He himself struggled with depression for much of his life. He wrote *The Principles of Psychology* in 1890, which met wide acclaim. Some, however, were critical of the tone of the work, such as psychologist Wilhelm Wundt, who called it "beautiful, but . . . not psychology."

The psychological philosophy known as functionalism, or functional philosophy, views mental life and behavior in relation to active adaptation to the person's environment. Functionalism gives a general basis for formulating psychological theories that are not testable by controlled experiments. Functionalism surfaced in the United States in the late 1800s in response to structuralism and later helped lead to behaviorism.

Contributions of Ivan Pavlov

Ivan Petrovich Pavlov, a Russian physiologist, is best known for his work in classical conditioning. He won the Nobel Prize for Physiology or Medicine in 1904. Pavlov's most famous concept is that of the conditioned reflex, which he developed in 1901. He learned this concept when examining salivation rates among dogs. Pavlov showed that when food being presented to a dog is done so in coordination with a bell or other sound, the dog would eventually learn to salivate without the presentation of the food and only with the sound. The idea of conditioning as an automatic form of learning became a key component to the school of behaviorism. Pavlov's work continues to have huge influence in modern behavior therapy.

Contributions of John Watson

John Broadus Watson was an American psychologist who established the psychological school of behaviorism. Watson conducted research on child rearing, advertising, and animal behavior through his behaviorist approach. His best-known research is the "Little Albert" experiment, which was quite controversial. In this experiment, Watson conditioned a small child to fear a white rat by pairing Albert's seeing the rat with a loud, frightening noise. They showed that this fear could be generalized to other white, furry objects. The ethical criticisms of this experiment include the fact that the young child was never deconditioned.

Watson's theories purported that the human mind began as a tabula rasa, or blank slate. He believed that one could mold an infant into any type of person one wanted—doctor, lawyer, beggar, or thief—regardless of the child's background and ancestry. He believed psychology should focus on observable behavior only, not on introspection.

Contributions of Sigmund Freud

Sigmund Freud was an Austrian neurologist, primarily known as the father of psychoanalysis, which is a clinical method for treating psychopathology through dialogue (between patient and psychoanalyst). Credited to Freud are therapeutic techniques such as free association as well as the discovery of transference. The primary theory underlying Freud's theory of psychoanalysis is the Oedipus complex. Dream analysis had a large role in Freud's practice and contributed to his theory of the unconscious as a disruptive force to the conscious state of mind.

In his theory of psychosocial development, Freud posits that psychological development in childhood occurs in a series of predetermined stages. He referred to these stages as "psychosexual stages" because (in his view) each stage represents the focus of libido (which he described as the drive for pleasure, not just sexual pleasure). As the child grows physically, different areas of his/her body become the focus of potential pleasure, frustration, or both. If a stage is not completed successfully, a child may become fixated on that particular part of the body or erogenous zone and will either over- or under-indulge in adulthood.

Freud's Psychosexual Developmental Stages

Oral stage (birth to 18 months). During this stage, a child focuses on oral pleasures (i.e., sucking). If the child has too much or too little oral gratification in this stage, it can result in an oral fixation, which is indicated by a preoccupation with oral activities (e.g., smoking, drinking, eating, or nail biting). Those who have an oral fixation or oral personality may be overly dependent on others, perpetual followers, and gullible. Conversely, it is also possible that they fight their urges and become pessimistic and aggressive toward others.

Anal stage (18 months to 3 years). The focus of pleasure during the anal stage is on eliminating and retaining feces. The child must learn to control anal stimulation by means of society's pressure (typically via the parents). Those adults with an anal fixation can have a preoccupation with cleanliness, perfection, and control. This is known as anal retentive. Conversely, they can also become messy and disorganized, which is known as anal expulsive.

Phallic stage (3 to 6 years). In this stage, the focus of pleasure is the genitals. Freud posited that in this stage, a boy develops unconscious sexual desires for his mother and consequently becomes rivals with his father, seeing him as competition for his mother's affection. He also is afraid of castration by his father as punishment for these feelings of desire. Freud named this phenomenon the Oedipus complex. Later, other thinkers added to the theory that girls go through a similar situation but with the genders reversed (i.e., having sexual feelings for their fathers). Freud disagreed with this, but it has been named the Electra complex by other psychoanalysts. Fixation in the phallic stage can cause sexual deviancies (of both avoidance and overindulgence) and weak or confused sexual identity.

Latency stage (6 years to puberty). During this stage, children's sexual urges are repressed, and they interact and play primarily with peers of the same sex.

Genital stage (puberty onward). This last stage of psychosexual development begins with puberty, when sexual urges are reawakened (after the latency stage). Adolescents direct their sexual urges onto opposite sex peers, and the primary focus of pleasure is the genitals.

Id, Ego, and Superego

Freud also posited that the human psyche has more than one facet. He saw the psyche as constructed of three parts: the id, ego, and superego. Each of these develops at different stages of life. These are not physical parts of the brain but rather psychological systems.

The most primitive and instinctive aspect of personality is the id. It is the impulsive and unconscious part of the psyche. It responds directly and immediately to instincts. The newborn child's personality is all id. The id operates on what Freud termed the pleasure principle, which is the notion that every desired impulse should be satisfied immediately without regard to the consequences. The id engages in primary process thinking (illogical, primitive, irrational, and fantasy).

The ego is id altered by the external world. It develops as a mediator between the unreality of the id and the external real world. It is the decision-making component of personality and works by reason in contrast to the chaos and unreason of the id. The ego functions on the reality principle and works out realistic ways of satisfying the demands of the id. The ego can compromise or postpone satisfaction to avoid negative consequences. The ego makes decisions based on societal norms, etiquette, and rules of behavior. Freud compared the ego to the rider of the id's horse. The ego tries to manage and steer the id's desires. It engages in secondary-process thinking (realistic, rational, and problem-solving) and develops in the phallic stage.

The superego seeks to control the impulses of the id, particularly those of sexuality and aggression. Additionally, it seeks to persuade the ego to rely on moralistic goals instead of merely realistic goals. The two systems of the superego are the conscience and the ideal self. It is through the conscious that the superego punishes the ego through feelings of guilt (i.e., if the ego gives into the id's demands). The ideal self, also called the ego ideal, is an imagined picture of how a person ought to be. It represents career aspirations, how one wishes to treat others, and how one wishes to behave as a part of society. If an individual's ideal self is an unrealistic standard, then the individual will see whatever he/she does as a failure. Parental values and upbringing determine the ideal self and conscience.

Jung

Carl Jung's work has influenced philosophy, anthropology, archaeology, literature, and religious studies in addition to psychiatry. Jung's theory of psychological types led to the development of the

- 22 -

Myers-Briggs Type Indicator, a highly popular personality test and psychometric instrument. Jung developed several important psychological concepts, which include the following:

- Introversion and extraversion (present-day definitions of these terms differ from the concepts he defined)
- The complex
- The collective unconscious
- Archetypes
- Individuation

Additionally, Jung was involved in spiritual concepts and believed that the journey of transformation (which he called individuation) is at the heart of all world religions. He defines this journey as a quest to meet the self and the divine. Jung is believed to have had an indirect role in the establishment of Alcoholics Anonymous due to his belief that spirituality could serve as a cure for alcoholism.

Although Jung held by Freud and his theories early on, they split after Jung publicly criticized Freud's theory of the Oedipus complex and how he emphasized the sexuality of the very young. Up to that point, their shared interest in the subconscious had brought Jung to support Freud. After separating from Freud, Jung later developed his own take on psychoanalytic theory. A significant portion of Jung's work reflects the theoretical differences that he had with Freud. For example, Jung asserted that libido was generalized psychic energy and not just sexual energy. Jung also believed that people are shaped by the future (i.e., their aspirations) as well as by the past and their childhood experiences.

Jung emphasized the unconscious more than Freud and proposed that the human psyche comprises three components—ego, personal unconscious, and collective unconscious. Jung's personal unconscious is analogous to Freud's unconscious. Jung's collective unconscious is a second, deeper layer that the individual shares with all other people. It comprises latent memories from our evolutionary and ancestral past. Jung referred to ancestral memories and images as archetypes and believed they are found in dreams, literature, art, and religion. Examples of important archetypes include the persona (social mask or public face), anima/animus (male and female sides), and the shadow (like Freud's id, animal urges, survival).

Piaget

When Jean Piaget's ideas became widely popularized in the 1960s, the designation of development as a major subfield of psychology soon followed. His cognitive development theory has four major stages:

1. Sensorimotor stage (birth to age 2)—In this stage, the child experiences the world through movement and his five senses. A child is extremely egocentric in this stage and cannot perceive the world from others' viewpoints. During the sensorimotor stage, children come to develop object permanence.
2. Preoperational stage (ages 2 to 7)—Beginning with the child's learning to speak, this stage sees an increase in children's playing and pretending, primarily through symbolic play and manipulating symbols. Children in this stage continue to have difficulty seeing things from different points of view. The two substages of the preoperational stage are the symbolic function substage and the intuitive thought substage.

3. Concrete operational stage (ages 7 to 11)—In this stage children are beginning to think logically and are no longer egocentric. They greatly improve their classification skills and become more aware of logic and conservation.
4. Formal operational stage (ages 11 to 16)—This stage sees the development of abstract reasoning. Children in this stage develop abstract thought and can conserve and think logically with more facility. Children in the formal operational stage show more skills for problem-solving.

Piaget posited that there are three types of intellectual structures:

- Behavioral (sensorimotor) schemata—organized patterns of behavior that represent and respond to objects and experiences
- Symbolic schemata—internal mental symbols, including images or verbal codes, used to represent aspects of experience
- Operational schemata—internal mental activity performed on objects of thought

As Piaget described them, schemata are significantly important building blocks of development and are modified by ongoing experiences. They are continuously being modified or changed and can be a generalized idea based on prior knowledge or experience.

Erikson

A student of Anna Freud (daughter to Sigmund Freud), Erik Erikson saw human development as continuing throughout the life span. This is in contrast to Freudian theory, which posits that development is mostly completed by adolescence. Erikson built onto the Freudian model of and extended it throughout the entire life span into older adulthood. Erikson appears to attempt a linkage between individual development and the broader context of society. His early stages are linked to those of Sigmund Freud, but they are formulated on different lines of thinking. Erikson focuses more on ego qualities that emerge from each stage and less on sexual modes and their consequences (as Freud's theory does).

The eight life stages of Erikson's theory of psychosocial development are as follows:

Basic Trust Versus. Basic Mistrust—the period of infancy (first year of life), also most fundamental stage. A baby develops a sense of trust based on the parental relationship. This sense of trust serves as a foundation for the child's sense of identity. Failure to develop basic trust results in feelings of fear and that the world is unpredictable and inconsistent.

Autonomy Versus Shame—early childhood, 1 to 3 years old (approx.). In this stage the child attempts to master toilet training.

Purpose (Initiative) Versus Guilt—preschool, 3 to 6 years old (approx.). The child learns to do things on his/her own, such as dressing. Feelings of guilt about making his/her own choices can be overshadowed by a positive sense of accomplishment.

Competence (Industry) Versus Inferiority—6 to 11 years (approx.). In this stage the child compares self-worth to others and can recognize inequalities in personal abilities among peers.

Identity (Fidelity) Versus Role Confusion—adolescence, 12 to 18 years (approx.). The adolescent questions self: Who am I? How do I fit in? Where am I going in life? Per Erikson, if parents push conformity to their own views on the adolescent, he/she will face identity confusion, but if parents allow exploration, he/she will assume his/her own identity.

Intimacy Versus Isolation—early adulthood, 18 to 35 (approx.). The individual experiences love and intimacy through successfully forming loving relationships with others (dating, marriage, friends, and family). If the individual is unable to form lasting relationships, he/she may feel isolated and alone.

Generativity Versus Stagnation—middle adulthood, ages 35 to 64 (approximately). In this stage, some settling into one's own life often occurs. The individual makes progress in a career or determines he/she unsure if about continuing in his/her path. Also important in this stage can be raising of children and/or participation in other meaningful activities. Those uncomfortable with the way their lives are progressing may feel regret and a sense of uselessness.

Ego Integrity Versus Despair—older adulthood, age 65 on (approximately). Individuals approach and/or achieve retirement and the last chapter of life. Ego integrity signifies the acceptance of one's life in its fullness, both accomplishments and defeats.

Skinner

B. F. Skinner was an American psychologist who developed a philosophy that he called radical behaviorism. He believed that free will in human beings is an illusion and that all human actions come about as a result of consequences. With bad consequences, the action may be repeated. With good consequences, it is more likely the action will be more likely. This is what Skinner named the principle of reinforcement. Skinner accepted thoughts and emotions as subject to the same rules as overt behavior. This is in contrast to methodological behaviorism, which does not accept so-called private events such as thinking and unobservable emotions as causes of a being's behavior.

Maslow

Abraham Maslow sought to understand the motivations that drive people. He believed that human beings are motivated by systems other than those related to rewards or unconscious desires. Maslow developed a hierarchy of needs that he believed motivate human beings. Before a person can progress to higher-level growth needs, he/she must satisfy the lower-level, more basic needs. Different life experiences, such as loss or illness may cause a person to move between the different levels of the hierarchy. The highest level in Maslow's model is that of self-actualization. Maslow asserted that only one in 100 people become fully self-actualized because of society's focus on lower needs such as esteem, love, and other social needs.

Maslow's first hierarchical model included five levels as follows:

1. Biological and physiological needs (air, food, drink, shelter, and sleep)
2. Safety needs (security and stability)
3. Love and belongingness needs (friendship, intimacy, and love)
4. Esteem needs (independence, status, achievement, self-respect, and respect of others)
5. Self-actualization needs (self-fulfillment, personal growth, and realizing personal potential)

Maslow later expanded this five-stage model to include cognitive, aesthetic, and transcendence needs. The eight-level model is as follows:

1. Biological and physiological needs
2. Safety needs
3. Love and belongingness needs
4. Esteem needs
5. Cognitive needs (knowledge and meaning)

6. Aesthetic needs (appreciation and search for balance, beauty, etc.)
7. Self-actualization needs
8. Transcendence needs (helping others achieve self-actualization)

Maslow's focus on human potential and how human beings fulfill that potential led him to focus on more positive aspects of human behavior instead of psychopathology. Maslow believed a person continues "becoming" always with a need for personal growth and discovery present throughout life. He saw self-actualization as a continual process of "becoming" more than a perfect state that one may reach. Self-actualization is achieving one's potential, not being perfect. Maslow studied people he considered to be self-actualized (including Einstein and Abraham Lincoln), and he identified 15 characteristics of a self-actualized person. They are as follows:

1. Ability to perceive reality efficiently and tolerate uncertainty
2. Acceptance of self and others for what they are
3. Spontaneity in thought and action
4. Problem centered rather than self-centered
5. Sense of humor
6. Ability to view life objectively
7. High level of creativity
8. Resistant to greater culture, however, not purposely unconventional
9. Concerned for humanity's welfare
10. Capable of deeply appreciating basic life experience
11. Able to establish deep, satisfying relationships with a few people
12. Peak experiences
13. Need for privacy
14. Democratic attitude
15. Strong moral and ethical standards

Maslow identified the following behaviors that he believed lead to self-actualization:

- Childlike ability to experience life and to fully absorb and concentrate
- Willingness to try new things and not just stay with safe options
- In evaluating experiences, listening to one's own feelings instead of the voice of the majority, of tradition, or of authority
- Being honest and avoiding pretense
- Willingness to be unpopular if one's views do not line up with those of the majority
- Working hard and taking responsibility
- Identifying one's own defenses and being willing and courageous enough to give them up

Bandura

Albert Bandura originated social learning theory as well as the theoretical construct of self-efficacy. Social learning theory explains that people can learn not only through direct experience but also through observing others. He conducted the significant Bobo doll experiment. This was actually a collection of experiments in 1961 and 1963 in which he studied the behavior of children after they watched an adult model behave aggressively toward a Bobo doll. The most noteworthy of these experiments measured the behavior of the children who observed the adult model beat up the Bobo doll and then be rewarded, punished, or face no consequence. This series of experiments show that humans can learn through observing, imitating, and modeling and that they can learn by watching others face consequences (reward or punishment) and not solely by experiencing consequences themselves, as behaviorism posits.

Major Principles of Social Learning Theory

- Learning is not solely behavioral but rather a cognitive process taking place in a social context.
- Learning can occur by vicarious reinforcement, which is observing a behavior and its consequences.
- Learning includes making observations, extracting information from said observations, and coming to a decision about the performance of the behavior. Consequently, learning can take place without an observable change in behavior.
- Reinforcement is not entirely responsible for learning but does play a role in learning.
- Learning is an active process, and cognition, environment, and behavior all reciprocally influence one another.

Types of Modeling Stimuli

- Live model
- Verbal instruction
- Symbolic (i.e., through media such as television, Internet, etc., and can utilize real or fictional characters)

Bandura's Cognitive and Behavioral Processes Necessary for Learning

- Attention, which is affected both by characteristics of the observer (perceptual abilities, cognitive abilities, arousal, and past performance) and characteristics of the event (relevance, novelty, affective valence, and functional value)
- Retention, also affected by both the characteristics of the observer (cognitive abilities and cognitive rehearsal), and characteristics of the event (complexity)
- Reproduction, affected by observer characteristics of physical and cognitive capabilities and previous performance
- Motivation, including predicted consequences and internal values

Independent Variable and Dependent Variable

The independent variable is also referred to as the experimental variable. This is the variable that will change based on the experimental treatment. For example, in a study on academic interventions, the independent variable includes a traditional curriculum and a new academic curriculum. The dependent variable is the variable that is measured based on the independent variable. In this example the dependent variable may be academic performance, which will be measured based on which group the student is in—the traditional curriculum or the new academic curriculum group. In other words, the researcher seeks to find differences in the dependent variable (academic performance) based on which group the participants are in (independent variable: traditional vs. new curriculum). Therefore, if students perform better when placed in the new academic curriculum group compared to those in the traditional curriculum group, the researcher may determine that the new curriculum is more effective.

Sampling Techniques

Sampling is an efficient method to investigate an entire population. The researcher gathers data on a small part of the whole population. This is called a sampling frame and is used to inform what the data looks like for the whole population. What follows are different types of sampling techniques:

- *Simple random sampling.* Researchers choose a random sample through methods that ensure that each subgroup of the whole population has an equal probability of being chosen as part of the sample.
- *Stratified random sampling.* Researchers divide the whole population into sections or strata. The researchers then choose a random sample from each. These are then combined into the overall sample.
- *Multi-stage sampling.* Researchers use this method when a population is too large and/or scattered to be practical to make a list from which to draw a simple random sample. Researchers may have to break the population down by variables to take random samples from each.

Examples of non-probability sampling techniques include voluntary response sampling, judgment sampling, and convenience sampling. Probability and statistics cannot be used to analyze the results of these types of techniques.

Operational Definitions

Operational definitions are the researchers' specific definitions about the variable tested in an investigation. Specifically, for a variable to be operationally defined, the researcher must include information about the procedure used to determine the variable. For example, if a variable is low socioeconomic status, the operational variable may be that low socioeconomic status includes all individuals who fall under the poverty line according to the Department of Housing and Urban Development. It is important to define variables in such a way that future researchers can replicate the study. Using well-defined operational definitions will also increase the validity and reliability of a study.

Common Research Concepts

- *Experimental study* changes one variable in the environment.
- *Observational study* tries to change as little of the existing environment as possible.
- *Longitudinal study* observes a large group of individuals who were born around the same time over a long period of time.
- *Cross-sectional study* observes individuals of different ages.
- *Cross-sequential study* combines both longitudinal and cross-sectional methodologies by observing different age groups over a long period of time and noting both similarities and differences in and between the groups.
- *Correlational study* establishes if two variables are correlated or not. Three types of correlations that can be identified are positive correlation (increase in one variable leads to an increase in the other and vice versa), negative correlation (increase in one variable leads to a decrease in another and vice versa), or no correlation.
- *Survey research* includes any research methods that involve asking questions of respondents from short written feedback to in-depth interviews.
- *Double blind procedure* is one in which neither the participants nor the experimenter are aware of which group the participant is in.

- Placebo affect occurs when an individual who is given a placebo and is unaware of that fact experiences changes that are similar to those experienced by individuals given the actual treatment.
- *Experimental group* is the research group that is given the actual treatment.
- *Control group* is the research group that is given no treatment or is given a placebo. For example, in this study on depression and medication, the experimental group will be given the study drug to examine the effects of this trend on depressive symptoms. The control group will be given either a placebo or no drug and all. In a double blind procedure, neither the participant nor the researcher will know who received the actual drug.
- *Case study* is an in-depth exploration into one individual or entity to gather as much information as possible to support or develop a theory or support the hypothesis. Case studies are beneficial in exploring situations that may not be widespread. For example, research involving brain damage is often done through case studies because there is not a large sample population of individuals with brain damage to draw from. One limitation of case studies is that they cannot be generalized to a larger population. Similarly, characteristics of an individual from a case study cannot be generalized to another individual with a similar issue (e.g., two people with right hemisphere brain damage). The reason for this is because the case study could be an atypical case.

Mode, Median, and Mean of Statistical Scores

Mode is a frequency score and is the most common score among all participants. For example, if a study measures academic performance, and five students receive an A, seven students receive a B, two students receive a C, and one student receives a D, the mode for this statistical data set is B as this was the most frequent score achieved. Median is the middle point at which all scores are lined sequentially from smallest two largest. For example, if the total score possible on a test is a 5, and 10 students obtained the following scores; 1, 1, 3, 3, 3, 4, 4, 4, 4, 5, the median score is a 4 because the score is located at the midpoint. Mean is the average of all scores. In the above example, the mean score is a 3.2.

Correlation

Correlation is the extent to which two things are related to each other. For example, research may suggest that minutes spent reading per day is correlated to academic performance. In stating this correlation, the researcher will aim to obtain a correlation coefficient that states the degree to which two things are correlated as well as the direction, which may be positive or negative. For example, if two items have a positive correlation, that means as one increases, the other increases as well. On the other hand, if two items have a negative correlation, it means as one increases, the other decreases. For example, if minutes spent reading per day and academic performance are positively correlated, this means the more time a child spends reading, the better his/her academic performance. Likewise, stress in the home is negatively correlated with academic performance; therefore, the more stress a child experiences at home, the more academic performance will decrease.

Measures of Variation

Range refers to the difference between the lowest and the highest score. For example, if the lowest score is a 70 and the highest score is the 100, the range of scores is 30. Standard deviation refers to the amount that one score defers or deviates from another score. This measure of variation tells the researcher if scores of an entire sample population are close together or widely disbursed. For example, a standard deviation of one indicates that one score typically defers from another by only plus or minus. As such, by looking at one score of 85, the researcher can be certain to find similar scores of 84 and 85. Normal curve, also referred to as an inverted U-shaped curve, indicates that most scores will fall within the middle, and fewer scores fall on the upper and lower points. For example, IQ is often indicated by a normal curve with the majority of people scoring at the midpoint, or around 100, and fewer people scoring either below or above this midpoint.

Ethical Considerations When Conducting Psychological Research

All researchers must first provide participants with an informed consent form that they must read and sign prior to beginning any psychological research. Contained within this form is information about the study, their responsibilities during the study, the researchers' responsibilities, information on confidentiality, as well a disclosure that the participant may quit the study without any negative repercussions. The researcher must also do everything possible to protect participants from harm. Researchers must maintain the confidentiality of all participants, which includes avoiding linking individual names or other identifying information to their study results. Finally, the researcher must fully debrief participants following the conclusion of the study. This includes providing them with any information that was not disclosed prior to beginning of the study as well as a brief discussion on the purpose of the study and what the results may be used for in the future.

Development of Ethical Principles in Research

There have been a number of important research studies that have influenced the development of ethical principles for research, for example, the Tuskegee Syphilis Study, conducted in the United States between 1932 and 1972. In this study, 400 African American men were left untreated for syphilis, even after penicillin became a proven treatment. The men were never told their diagnosis. Between 1939 and 1945 Nazi scientists conducted experiments on prisoners in concentration camps. The Nuremberg Code for research on human subjects was adopted after the end of World War II and was subsequently used to convict Nazi scientists of war crimes. The Obedience to Authority Study, published in 1974 by Stanley Milgram, proved that many people will do things they consider to be wrong morally if they are following an authority's orders. The World Medical Association's Helsinki Declaration established ethical principles for research on human subjects. The National Research Act was passed by the U.S. Congress in 1974 and authorized federal agencies to develop human research regulations.

Assessment

Through psychological assessment, psychologists use a combination of techniques to come to a conclusion about a person and his/her behavior and/or personality and capabilities. This is also called psychological testing or performing a psychological battery. Reliability is the extent to which an assessment instrument produces consistent and stable results. Validity is how well an assessment measures what it claims to measure. Psychological assessment should take place under standardized conditions with each person being assessed under basically identical conditions. Standardization is important because many test results are used to compare performance among participants. Assessment norms consist of data that enable the assessors to establish the relative standing of an individual person who has been assessed. A test score on its own means little. Usually, assessors must interpret a test score to determine one's position relative to others who have been assessed. Norms offer a basis to compare the individual within the group.

Limits of Psychological Assessment

Although psychological assessments can be useful, they do all have some limitations. One should take into account the way that the assessment tool is constructed. For example, some assessment tools rely heavily on the interpretation of the assessor and not on objective results. Other tests measure attributes not based on science, such as personality types. Another limitation of assessments can come through cultural bias. Many tests make assumptions of those being assessed, for example, that those being assessed will have similar experiences and language proficiency in English. Different cultures (even within one country, such as the United States) vary widely, and individuals from different cultures (majority culture, minority cultures) will likely interpret items in a psychological assessment quite differently due to upbringing and cultural perspectives. This can cause inaccuracies in the results. Another limitation of psychological assessments comes from the participants themselves, who may not give true responses. Some respondents may try to portray themselves in a more positive light and will distort their answers accordingly. A final limitation comes in the interpretation of the results. Assessors can make errors, even those with much skill and experience. This is more likely when the assessment involves either emotional or cognitive responses. These are more likely to get a subjective interpretation, and the same response may be scored differently depending on who the assessor is.

Parts of the Neuron

- Dendrites extend away from the body of the neuron cell to receive messages from other neurons at synapses. They are somewhat treelike in structure, and not all neurons have them.
- Synapses allow the dendrites from a particular neuron to receive signals from and interact with other neurons.
- Axons send signals to other neurons, organs, or muscles and are tubelike in structure. Not all neurons have them.
- The soma is where the signals from the dendrites are linked and sent on. Along with the nucleus, the soma helps maintain the cell and keep it functional.
- Mitochondria are a support structure for the neuron that provide energy for it.
- The Golgi apparatus packages products created by the neuron and secretes them outside the cell wall.

Action Potential

A part of the process that happens during the firing of a neuron is called an action potential. During this process, part of the neural membrane opens and allows positively charged ions inside the cell and negatively charged ions out. Through this process, there is a quick increase in the positive charge of the nerve fiber. When this positive charge is high enough, the impulse is spread down the nerve fiber. The nerve carries this electric impulse down throughout itself through a series of these action potentials.

Types of Neurons

- Neuromodulators moderate circuits or regions of the brain by affecting a group of neurons and thus causing a modulation of that group. Some neuromodulators act as neurotransmitters.
- Neurotransmitters affect only one other neuron. This can be called a neuron-to-neuron exchange of information. They are chemicals used to relay, modulate, and amplify electric signals between a neuron and another cell. If a chemical meets all of the following conditions, it can be classified as a neurotransmitter:
  - Synthesized endogenously (within the presynaptic neuron)

- 31 -

- o Available in adequate quantity in the presynaptic neuron to cause an effect on the post synaptic neuron
  - o Externally administered and mimics the endogenously released substance
  - o Present biochemical mechanism for inactivation
- A ganglion is a group of neuromodulators. There are 32 pairs of ganglion throughout the human body to control all autonomic and somatic actions.
- Sensory neurons travel from the organs of the body to the brain to relay information related to the five senses.
- Motor neurons that travel from the brain back down to the organs of the body with the response based on the information the sensory neuron sent.
- Interneurons are located within the brain and serve as an internal communication system from one part of the brain to another.

Types of Neurotransmitters

- Acetylcholine works on muscle functioning, learning, and memory. It is present at all neuro synapses surrounding the skeletal muscles and is released when muscles contract.
- Dopamine is responsible for learning, attention, and emotion, as well as movement. It is necessary for the normal functioning of the brain, and too much or too little dopamine may result in physical and psychological problems. Too much dopamine (either naturally or due to drug use) can cause suspicious personality, paranoia, and withdrawal from social situations. A buildup of dopamine (such as from amphetamines or cocaine) can lead to drug-induced psychosis or schizophrenia. Too little dopamine can cause difficulty in movement and conditions such as Parkinson's.
- Serotonin strongly influences arousal, mood, sleep, and hunger. It is believed that too little of it has a role in causing depression. Too much can cause excessive nerve cell activity and a possibly deadly collection of symptoms referred to as serotonin syndrome.

Organization of the Nervous System

The nervous system is the communication network between the organs of the body and the brain. This system consists of nerve cells that send chemical impulses from organs to the brain to receive information on how to respond to stimuli. The two main subsystems of the nervous system include the central nervous system (CNS) and the peripheral nervous system (PNS). The central nervous system includes the spine and brain, and the peripheral nervous system includes all organs and areas of the body outside of the spine and brain.

The sympathetic nervous system works to initiate the appropriate functions for action. In other words, the sympathetic nervous system will arouse the body in times of stress. Conversely, the parasympathetic nervous system acts to conserve energy and will calm the body during times of rest.

The somatic nervous system is a part of the peripheral nervous system and controls all skeletal muscles. The autonomic nervous system is also part of the peripheral nervous system; however, this system controls the internal organs of the body and the glands. Additionally, the autonomic nervous system serves two functions; on the sympathetic side, arousal occurs, and on the parasympathetic side, an inhibition or a calming effect occurs.

Lobes of the Brain

The brain is divided into four main lobes: the frontal lobe, the parietal lobe, the occipital lobe, and the temporal lobes. The frontal lobe located in the front of the brain is responsible for short-term and working memory and information processing as well as decision-making, planning, and judgment. The parietal lobe is located slightly toward the back of the brain and the top of the head and is responsible for sensory input as well as spatial positioning of the body. The occipital lobe is located at the back of the head just above the brain stem. This lobe is responsible for visual input, processing, and output; specifically, nerves from the eyes enter directly into this lobe. Finally, the temporal lobes are located at the left and right sides of the brain. These lobes are responsible for all auditory input, processing, and output.

Motor Cortex and Sensory Cortex

The motor cortex is located near the back of the frontal lobes and is responsible for voluntary movement. Of note, the hemispheres of the brain control the opposite side of the body; therefore, the left side of the motor cortex will control the right side of the body and vice versa. The sensory cortex is located at the front of the parietal lobes and is responsible for the input and processing of touch and other sensations related to movement. Those body parts that are more sensitive are correlated to a larger area of the sensory cortex.

Audio Cortex, Visual Cortex, and Motor Cortex in Speech Processing

The audio cortex, also referred to as Wernicke's area, processes all audio information. This area is located in the temporal lobe of the brain and is involved in the understanding of information. Damage in this area of the brain results in a deficiency in being able to read a word from a page or explain the events depicted in a picture. Once processed through the audio cortex, information passes to the visual cortex, also called the angular gyrus located in the occipital lobe, where the person sees or visualizes the word. The angular gyrus is also essential to reading aloud, and damage to this area of the brain will affect this function. Finally, information is sent to be processed in the motor cortex, or Broca's area. Once information is processed, the individual will respond appropriately. Broca's area is key in speech; therefore, damage to this area will affect the individual's response to processed information.

Hemispheres of the Brain, Corpus Callosum, and Lateralization

The brain is divided into two hemispheres down the middle, and each hemisphere appears to specialize in certain functions. That each hemisphere has different functions is called the lateralization theory. The two sides communicate with each other through a band of fibers called the corpus callosum. The corpus callosum consists of a number of fibrous nerves that are gathered in a band and stretch from the left hemisphere to the right hemisphere. This band of fibers passes information from one side of the brain to the other, allowing the brain in the left and right sides of the body to coordinate and function as one. In cases of a split brain, the corpus callosum is severed, inhibiting the individual to coordinate left and right hemisphere processes. For example, when presented with the word *car* in the right visual field, an individual with a split brain will be able to draw the word, however, will not be able to read the word. This is because information in the right visual field is processed on the left side of the brain, which is responsible for verbal activities; conversely, the right side of the brain is responsible for visual and artistic activities, and therefore the individual can draw the picture.

- 33 -

Limbic System

The limbic system is a collection of structures in the brain that controls basic emotions (e.g., pleasure and fear) and drives (e.g., hunger and sex). The four main structures of the limbic system are the amygdala, the hippocampus (important in memory and learning), regions of the limbic cortex, and the septal area. The limbic system is connected to the hypothalamus, thalamus, and cerebral cortex. Functions associated with the limbic system include learning, behavior, sense of smell, emotions, long-term memory, and drives. The limbic system influences other systems, including the endocrine system and the autonomic nervous system, and is linked to the prefrontal cortex and the pleasure center of the brain.

Cerebellum, Thalamus, and Hypothalamus

The cerebellum is a part of the brain that appears to be a separate structure located at the bottom of the brain. It plays an important role in motor control and possibly in some cognitive functions such as attention and language or also in regulating fear or pleasure responses. The cerebellum does not set off the process of movement but is key to coordination and timing. The thalamus is located at the top of the brain stem and serves as the center for sensory information processing. The thalamus receives and processes information from every sense except smell. The hypothalamus is located below the thalamus, serves as the manager of the endocrine system, and monitors basic needs including hunger, thirst, and sleep.

Methods for Studying the Brain

- Positron emission tomography (PET) evaluates the metabolism of the brain to glean information about its physiology and anatomy as well as its biochemical properties. PET is able to discover biochemical changes before other tests (which rely on only studying anatomical changes). To conduct a PET scan on the brain, radionuclides are formed by attaching a radioactive atom to glucose as this is the substance the brain uses for its metabolism. The activity of the glucose can then be observed.
- Magnetic resonance imaging (MRI) provides a picture of the soft tissue of the brain via magnetic fields and the radio waves produced by the brain during a given task.
- Functional MRI (fMRI) reveals brain function by visualizing the blood flow over a series of MRI images while the individual performs tasks. Uses of fMRI include examining the brain's anatomy; brain mapping (i.e., to determine which part of the brain handles critical functions such as thought, speech, etc.); assessing the effects of trauma, stroke, or degenerative disease on brain function; monitoring brain tumors, and guiding planning for surgery or radiation therapy.
- Electroencephalogram (EEG) detects the brain's electrical activity using electrodes attached to the scalp. Brain cells are always active and communicate through electrical impulses. The EEG can measure these impulses and is one of the primary diagnostic tests for epilepsy. It also plays a role in diagnosing other brain disorders. During the EEG, different stimuli will be presented to the individual to activate different brain waves.

Adrenal Glands

The adrenal glands are located above the kidneys and generate a wide variety of hormones. They are made of several different layers that all affect the composition and function of the glands. Each adrenal gland consists of an outer cortex that surrounds a core of medulla. The adrenal cortex creates a type of steroid hormones called corticosteroids. These corticosteroids include mineralocorticoids (which help in blood pressure regulation and balance of electrolytes). Another type is glucocorticoids, like cortisol, that helps regulate glycogen, lipometabolism, and suppression of the immune system. The internal layer of the adrenal cortex generates androgens, which the gonads convert to fully functional sex hormones. The medulla produces epinephrine and norepinephrine, which work in the fight-or-flight response to increase the body's arousal in stressful situations.

Pituitary Gland

The pituitary gland is possibly the most important part of the endocrine system and is called the "master gland" as it controls several other of the hormone-producing glands, such as the thyroid and the adrenals. It sits behind the bridge of the nose, just below the base of the brain and is generally about the size of a pea. It has two parts, or lobes, the anterior pituitary and the posterior pituitary. The hormones that the pituitary gland produces control the functions of other endocrine glands. Several important hormones are produced by the anterior pituitary such as growth hormone, gonadotrophins (which are part of the puberty process), thyroid-stimulating hormone, prolactin, and adrenocorticotrophic hormone (ACTH). The posterior pituitary produces a hormone that balances fluid called anti-diuretic hormone (ADH).

Thyroid and Parathyroid Glands

The thyroid is located along the front of the windpipe, just below the Adam's apple and is a butterfly-shaped gland. It has two lobes connected by a bridge between them. The thyroid cannot be felt when it is its normal size. Thyroid hormones include thyroxine, or T4, and triiodothyronine, or T3. They are primarily responsible for metabolism regulation. Thyroid hormones also influence growth, development, and body temperature and are crucial for brain development in infancy and childhood.

The parathyroid glands are four small glands usually situated on the back of the thyroid. Along with calcitonin (which is produced by the thyroid) parathyroid hormone plays a key role in regulating the amount of calcium in the bones and blood.

Pancreas

The pancreas is located in the abdominal cavity just behind the stomach and is a part of both the digestive and endocrine systems. It produces several hormones, which include insulin, glucagon, somatostatin, and pancreatic polypeptide.

Testes

Otherwise known as gonads, the testes (testicles) produce sperm and maintain the health of the male reproductive system. Testes also secrete testosterone, a hormone that is critical to the development of male physical characteristics. It is necessary for the healthy development of male sex organs, growth of facial and body hair, vocal changes, increase in height and muscle mass, and growth of the Adam's apple. In adult males, testosterone maintains muscle strength, bone density, and libido.

Ovaries

The ovaries produce three major estrogens—estradiol, estrone, and estriol—that work together toward the healthy development of female sex characteristics during puberty and afterward to ensure fertility. These help in breast development; fat distribution in the legs, breasts, and hips; and development of reproductive organs. Other hormones produced by the ovaries are relaxin, which is

- 35 -

released prior to giving birth, and inhibin, which communicates to the pituitary to inhibit follicle-stimulating hormone secretion. Close to the end of pregnancy, the pituitary gland is alerted by increased estrogen levels to release oxytocin, which causes uterine contractions to begin.

Other Hormones

Melatonin is involved in the entrainment of circadian rhythms for physiological functions such as sleep. It is produced by the pineal gland in darkness, therefore typically at night. The pineal gland is found in the center of the brain, outside the blood-brain barrier.

Serotonin acts as a neurotransmitter and controls mood, appetite, and sleep cycles. It impacts some cognitive functions such as memory and learning. It is manufactured in the brain where its primary functions are performed, however, about 90% of the serotonin in the human body is in the digestive tract and blood platelets.

Dopamine helps regulate movement and emotional responses and also controls the heart rate. It also aids in perception, helping one to determine what is and isn't real. It is a neurotransmitter that helps manage the reward and pleasure centers in the brain. Low dopamine activity may be indicated in a person being more prone to addiction. Dopamine deficiency leads to Parkinson's disease. People known as risk takers, who tend to be sensation seekers, often have a certain type of dopamine receptor that others do not.

Growth hormone is produced by the pituitary gland and is the catalyst for growth in children and adolescents. It helps stimulate the growth and reproduction of cells in the body. Growth hormone also helps regulate body fluids, muscle growth, bone growth, metabolism of fat and sugar, and possibly heart function.

Leptin speeds up metabolism while concurrently slowing down the appetite.

Orexin increases alertness and energy levels and also increases appetite.

Nature Versus Nurture

Nature versus nurture is the idea that some of a person's traits result from genetic heritage and some result from environment. In this context, nature refers to any trait that an individual is born with or has acquired through genes. Nurture may be seen as the opposite of nature; it refers to any trait that an individual acquires from the environment. Nurture often refers specifically to the environment created by the parents of the child, but it can refer to any environmental condition that affects development. Historically, some philosophers have believed that the mind is a blank slate (tabula rasa) that requires experience and learning to develop. In contrast, other thinkers have purported that all of a person's characteristics are set at birth. Most psychologists today believe that the development of a human being is affected by both biology and experience.

Evolutionary Psychology

Evolutionary psychology is an approach that seeks to explain cognitive and psychological traits as the product of natural selection. Its focus is on how the processes of evolution have shaped the human mind and behavior. Examples of psychological adaptations that evolutionary psychology claims to explain are language acquisition, incest avoidance, intelligence, and so on. The roots of evolutionary psychology are in both cognitive psychology and evolutionary biology.

Sensory Adaptation

Sensory adaptation is a phenomenon that occurs after a person is presented with a stimulus over a period of time, and his/her senses no longer perceive the stimulus but rather have become adapted to it. For example, when going from a dark room to a bright room our eyes receive intense sensory information from the light, which results in the desire to squint. However, after a short period of time, our eyes adapt to the light, no longer perceiving the light as threatening or too bright, and squinting is no longer needed. Sensory adaptation is necessary so that the information processing systems within our brains do not go into sensory overload. After a short period of time of adjustment, our attention can tune out some stimuli and focus on more important input.

Feature Detection and Parallel Processing

Feature detection refers to a process in which the nervous system can filter or sort complex stimuli so that one can extract significant characteristics that are more likely to belong to important objects. This process allows the brain to filter out more irrelevant or background stimuli. Parallel processing is the phenomenon in which the brain is able to concurrently process incoming stimuli of varying quality and importance.

Place Theory

Place theory proposed by Hermann von Helmholtz states that an individual's ability to hear pitch is the result of sound waves stimulating different parts of the cochlea basilar membrane. This theory suggests it is not necessarily the sound or the pitch that the brain is processing but rather the place at which the stimulus hits the ear. This theory was supported through research that found that the cochlea vibrates in different places depending on the pitch of a sound. For example, the higher-frequency pitches vibrated the beginning of the cochlea membrane, whereas lower-frequency pitches vibrated the end of the cochlea membrane. It is important to note, however, that lower-frequency pitches do not always vibrate only the end of the cochlea membrane, and therefore this theory does not fully explain them.

Frequency Theory

Frequency theory suggests that an individual can perceive pitch based on the frequency of the pitch. When the sound waves of a pitch enter the ear, they have different effects, depending on their frequency, on the nerves surrounding the ear, creating different nerve impulses that travel to the brain. Based on these nerve impulses, the brain will perceive the pitch as high or low. Frequency theory provides a thorough explanation of how individuals perceive low-level pitches; however, it does not provide a comprehensive explanation for higher-pitched frequencies. Specifically, as neurons are unable to fire more than 1,000 times per second, this theory does not address pitch frequencies that require impulses above that rate, as some higher-pitched frequencies do.

Difference Threshold and Webster's Law

The difference threshold is the point at which an individual can detect differences in a stimulus at least 50% of the time. An example of a difference threshold would be when holding a weight of, for example, 100 ounces. To determine the difference threshold, small additions will be made, for example, 5 ounces at a time until the individual notices a difference in the weight. The difference threshold may depend on a number of factors, but the primary factor that will determine difference threshold is explained by Webster's law. Webster's law states that the proportion of two different stimuli must be equal to determine an adequate difference threshold. For example, whereas holding 100 ounces and adding 5 ounces at a time will result in one difference threshold, holding 1,000 ounces and adding 5 ounces at a time will result in a different difference threshold. However, the difference thresholds between the two cases will be equal if 50 ounces is added at a time to the 1,000 ounces being held.

Absolute Threshold

Absolute threshold refers to the amount or intensity that is required of a stimulus for an individual to perceive it at least 50% of the time. The absolute threshold will vary depending on age, experience, and environment. For example, older individuals may have a higher absolute threshold for hearing than younger individuals due to hearing loss associated with aging. Another example is the variance an absolute threshold may have depending on the environment that the individual is in. For example, if an individual is in complete darkness his/her absolute threshold for hearing may be lower than when the individual is in the light because a sense of hearing will be heightened in the absence of a sense of light.

Visual Sensory System

The visual sensory system allows humans to understand their environment through detecting and interpreting light. The eye receives light rays and changes them into a form that the brain can understand, that is, electrical and chemical signals. This is a process known as phototransduction. The brain decodes these chemical and electrical signals and forms images from them. There are three basic layers, known as tunics, in the human eye. The outermost layer is the fibrous tunic and is made up of the sclera and the cornea. The middle layer is the vascular tunic and includes the iris and pupil. This layer provides oxygen to the rest of the eye and also removes waste through the many blood vessels it contains. The innermost layer is the nervous tunic, which includes the retina. This layer is receptive to light and connects to the brain via the optic nerve. The retina is the part of the eye that converts light into neural signals. It contains photoreceptor cells, which both sense and respond to light. The two types of photoreceptor cells are rods and cones. Rods work with low levels of light; they do not detect color. Cones need much more light, are much less numerous than rods, and detect color, sharpness, and detail.

Auditory Sensory System

The auditory system allows the brain to distinguish sounds and extract meaning from them. As in the visual system, the auditory system utilizes transduction but, in this case, to convert sound waves (vs. light waves in the visual system) into electrical impulses that the brain can decode. The outer ear includes the parts of the ear that are visible to the naked eye, called the pinna, as well as the auditory canal. The pinna help reflect sound into the auditory canal, which amplifies the sound. The eardrum, also known as the tympanic membrane, is at the end of the auditory canal. The middle ear includes everything from the inside of the eardrum to the outside of the oval window of the inner ear. The three tiny bones of the middle ear, or ossicles, are the malleus (hammer), incus (anvil), and stapes (stirrup). The ossicles transmit sound vibrations in air from the eardrum to sound vibrations in the fluid of the cochlea. The cochlea and the vestibular system form the inner ear. When the stapes vibrates on the oval window (the beginning of the inner ear), it causes movement in the fluid of the inner ear. The cochlea takes these fluid sound waves and converts them into nerve impulses, which can be understood by the brain. The vestibular system (see what follows for more detail), also in the inner ear, is made of semicircular canals and uses the same fluid and hair cells that the cochlea uses for sound but to manage balance and motion.

Olfactory System

The olfactory system, or the sense of smell, transmits information about the chemical composition of substances to the brain. Through olfaction, people are able to perceive substances in the environment. These substances can be airborne, in which case they are detected by the main olfactory system, or in liquid form, in which case the accessory olfactory system deals with them. The sense of smell aids in the discovery and recognition of hazardous substances as well as more pleasant substances, such as food or pheromones. It is also closely connected to memory due to its close neural connections with parts of the brain concerned with emotions and memory. This means that often a scent or fragrance can stimulate memories. Olfaction also greatly contributes to the sense of taste, or the gustatory system. Older adults often experience a loss of the sense of smell, often due to accumulated damage caused by viruses and other minor trauma.

Gustation

Gustation, or the sense of taste, works in similar ways to the olfactory system. Through chemoreception, the brain is able to interpret chemical compounds as flavors. There are five main types of taste sensation: sweet, salty, bitter, sour, and savory (also referred to as umami). Taste buds on the tongue include gustatory cells, which are also called taste receptor cells. Taste receptors are found around the papillae on the surface of the tongue, cheek, upper esophagus, epiglottis, and soft palate. Despite a myth that there are certain zones of the tongue devoted to each of the different types of taste, any taste on the tongue can detect any of the five types of taste. Around age 50, human beings experience a loss of tongue papillae and a reduction in production of saliva. This leads to a decrease in the sense of taste.

Somatosensory System

The sense of touch is otherwise known as the somatosensory system. There are sensory receptor cells throughout the entire body that help the individual to detect sensations and changes on the surface of the body or within it. Different stimuli activate the sensory receptor cells. These stimuli include temperature, pain, vibrations, texture, and movement. The somatosensory system also helps the individual understand where his/her body is in space and how it is moving, which is related to the vestibular and proprioception systems.

Vestibular and Proprioception Systems

Like the other senses, the vestibular system gathers information about the outside world and communicates it to the brain. The vestibular system manages balance and motion through the fluid and hair cells in the inner ear. It helps the individual to know which way is up or down and in which direction a person's body is moving. The vestibular system helps the brain compensate for eye and body movement so that it can understand what the person is seeing without all input being hopelessly blurred and confusing.

In contrast to the other sensory systems, proprioception does not gather information from the outside world to communicate it to the brain. Instead, it gathers information about the body itself from receptors in the muscles, tendons, joints, and fascia. Movement is often necessary to trigger these receptors. This is similar to the vestibular system, which also requires movement. The vestibular and proprioception systems cannot easily be separated as many movements and activities involve both systems.

Perceptual Set

The phrase *perceptual set* describes the inclination to view objects or situations from a specific frame of reference. Perceptual sets generally lead one to form reasonably accurate conclusions, which are heavily influenced by expectations and prior knowledge. Perceptual sets are often guided by schemas, mental frameworks, and concepts. One example is that of faces. Human beings have a strong schema for faces, which makes it easier to recognize human faces in the environment. This can also mean that when a person sees an ambiguous image, he/she is more likely to see it as a face than as another kind of object.

Figure Ground

Figure ground organization is the ability to identify a figure from the background. This is an important factor in recognizing objects visually. The three types of figure ground situations are those in which the figure and the ground compete, those in which the figure should be the ground and the ground should be the figure, and those in which the figure and the ground create an optical illusion.

Depth Perception

Depth perception allows human beings to perceive the world visually in three dimensions and also allows humans to perceive the distance of an object. Sources of information from the environment or within the body that help one perceive how far away an object is are called depth cues. Depth cues can fall into two categories: binocular, which requires use of both eyes, and monocular, which requires the use of only one eye. Monocular cues include size, texture, overlap, shading, height, and clarity. Binocular cues include convergence and retinal disparity. Convergence describes the phenomenon in which the closer an object is, the more inward one's eyes need to turn to focus. Retinal disparity refers to the fact that each eye sees a slightly different image and extracts distance information from each of them.

Constancy

Perceptual constancy can also be referred to as object constancy or constancy phenomenon and describes the tendency to see familiar objects as having a standard shape, size, or color, regardless of changes in the perspective angle, distance, or lighting. This makes people able to identify objects under various conditions; for example, snow is understood to be white whether in the low illumination of moonlight or in bright sunlight.

Selective Attention

Selective attention is the individual's ability to process only necessary information while additional and unnecessary information or stimuli is blocked out. This is important as individuals are presented with millions of pieces of information per second that they could not possibly process. One common example of selective attention is the cocktail party effect. This effect occurs when individuals are having a conversation in a crowded, noisy room. They are able to tune out the other conversations and focus on their single conversation because of selective attention. Although humans do have this ability, in situations where attention is necessary, engaging in other tasks may result in a focus of attention moving from one activity to the other. For example, while driving and talking on a cell phone, an individual's attention may shift to the conversation and tune out the road.

Selective Inattention

Selective inattention is the phenomenon that humans are inattentive to the majority of incoming stimuli. For example, when presented with a series of pictures with only a slight change, the majority of individuals will not notice the change. This can also be referred to as change blindness, which suggests that unless paying attention to a possible change in the setting or environment, the individual will not notice a difference. Inattentional blindness occurs when the individual does not notice objects unless paying specific attention to them. For example, if instructed to look for a dog in a picture, then asked if a cat was in the picture, the individual will likely not notice the cat because they were not attending to this object.

Consciousness

The awareness that people have of themselves and their environment is referred to as consciousness. William James posited that consciousness is a steady stream of thoughts, emotions, and perceptions. There are two main aspects to consciousness: monitor and control. The ability to perceive one's surroundings, identify potential problems, and make decisions is monitoring. Control describes the ability to organize thoughts and use behaviors to complete tasks.

Pre-consciousness

In the field of psychoanalysis, pre-consciousness describes thoughts that are not repressed but are unconscious at a particular moment. They are available for recall and can easily become conscious thoughts. Priming is one of the most common forms of preconscious processing. Priming describes an effect of implicit memory in which one is exposed to a stimulus, which in turn influences a response to a second stimulus. Perceptual, semantic, or conceptual stimuli can lead to priming. An example of priming is giving a person a list of words to read that includes the word *cabinet* and later asking the person to name a word that starts with *cab-*. The person will be more likely to answer with *cabinet* than if he/she were not primed. Other types of preconscious processing are the tip-of-the-tongue phenomenon and blindsight.

Altered States

An altered state of consciousness describes a mental state brought on by psychological, physiological, or pharmacological causes and deviates from the normal waking conscious state. They may be caused either intentionally or accidentally. Accidental altered states are generally considered pathological and include traumatic experiences, epilepsy, infections, oxygen deficiency, fasting, sleep deprivation, or psychosis. Intentional altered states are often recreational and are generally caused by pharmacological substances, such as MDMA (ecstasy), opiates, cocaine, or alcohol. Some altered states of consciousness can be caused by a combination of factors, for example a person with a psychiatric disorder who consumes psycho-active substances.

Stages of Sleep

Most individuals experience five stages of sleep, 1 through 4 and rapid eye movement (REM). Stages 1 through 4 are differentiated by the brain waves that are most active during that stage and include: beta, alpha, theta, and delta. Also associated with these four states of sleep are differences in muscle activity, temperature, and blood pressure. Beta waves are high-frequency waves (18–24 cycles/second) and are most prevalent while awake. Alpha waves are slower (8–12 cycles/second) and occur during states of relaxation. Theta waves occur every 4 to 7 cycles/second and indicate the transition from alpha, relaxation, to sleep (Stage 1). Stage 2 sleep occurs when the body falls into a deeper sleep and the body and brain continue to slow. Stages 3 and 4 are indicated by deep

- 41 -

sleep and delta waves. The final stage of sleep is referred to as REM sleep. It is during the REM period that dreaming occurs.

During REM sleep, breathing speeds up and becomes more irregular and shallow, limb muscles are temporarily paralyzed, and eyes jerk rapidly. Brain waves increase to levels like those when a person is awake. Blood pressure rises, heart rate increases, and the body loses some temperature regulation ability. Most people go through three to five REM intervals every night. Infants spend nearly half of their sleep time in REM sleep, whereas adults spend about half their sleep time in Stage 2, 20% in REM, and the rest divided between the other stages. As adults age, they will spend progressively less time in REM sleep.

Activation-Synthesis Theory

The activation-synthesis model states that brain activation during REM sleep results in synthesis of dream creation. It suggests that dreams are caused by the physiological processes of the brain when circuits in the brain stem are activated during REM sleep. Once they are activated, parts of the limbic system that deal with emotions, sensations, and memories become active. The brain then synthesizes and interprets all of this activity and seeks to create meaning from these signals, which results in dreaming. This model was developed by researchers J. Allan Hobson and Robert McCarley. Hobson has five dream characteristics, which are as follows: illogical content, intense emotions, acceptance of strange content, strange sensory experiences, and difficulty remembering content.

Dreams in Psychoanalytic Theory

Freud saw dreams as highly instructive and believed that they perform important functions for the unconscious mind and serve as valuable clues to how it operates. According to Freud, the manifest content of a dream is what the dreamer remembers, and the symbolic meaning is the latent content. Through a process called dream work, one can come to translate the underlying wish in the latent content.

Sleep Theories

There are theories that attempt to explain why we sleep. The adaptive or evolutionary theory proposes that being inactive at night helped keep our ancestors out of harm's way at times they would be more vulnerable. The energy conservation theory puts forward that sleep's primary function is to reduce the demand for energy expenditure, particularly at times that searching for food is less efficient. Another explanation can be referred to as the restorative theory and suggests that sleep is necessary for the body to repair and rejuvenate itself. Recent empirical evidence appears to support this theory as animals that are entirely deprived of sleep die in a matter of weeks. Specific restorative functions that sleep provides include muscle growth, tissue repair, protein synthesis, and growth hormone release. The brain plasticity theory purports that sleep is necessary for organization and growth of brain structures. Evidence of this theory can be seen in the negative effect that sleep deprivation has on people's ability to learn and perform tasks.

Psychoactive Drugs

A psychoactive drug can be any chemical substance that changes brain function and causes alterations in mood, perception, or consciousness. The main categories of psychoactive drugs are narcotics, depressants, stimulants, and hallucinogens. Other drugs that have psychoactive effects but do not fit into these categories are cannabis (marijuana) and steroids.

A person who uses a drug repeatedly may develop a tolerance to the drug. Sometimes larger and larger doses are needed to produce the same effect when a substance is used over a long period of time. Dependence describes factors that make it difficult for a person to stop using a drug. Dependence factors include craving and withdrawal. Dependence may be either psychological or physical. Addiction describes a chronic brain disease that causes compulsive substance use in spite of harmful consequences.

Drugs that cause psychological dependence typically produce one or more of the following effects: reduced tension/anxiety, elation/euphoria, feeling of a temporary escape from reality, altered perceptions, or feelings of increased mental or physical ability. Psychological dependence can lead to the user continuing to use the drug despite knowing it may be physically harmful or interferes with important parts of life, such as family or work.

If a drug causes physical dependence, stopping the use of that drug will result in unpleasant or even painful physical symptoms. These symptoms occur due to the body's adaptation to the continuous presence of the substance. Withdrawal describes the physical problems and emotions that a person experiences if he/she is dependent on a substance and then suddenly stops or greatly reduces intake of it. Withdrawal symptoms range from the mild to the life-threatening. A person in withdrawal may experience nausea, shakiness, sweating, extreme confusion, jumpiness, or hallucinations (auditory, visual, or tactile). Delirium tremens (DTs) can include all the aforementioned symptoms plus seizures. If untreated, delirium tremens can lead to death.

Narcotics

Narcotics are drugs that are used medicinally to relieve pain. They cause relaxation with an immediate rush, or high, and have a high potential for abuse. Their effects include restlessness, nausea, euphoria, drowsiness, respiratory depression, and constricted pupils. Examples of narcotics include morphine, heroin, oxycodone, and fentanyl.

Depressants

Depressants are used medicinally to relieve anxiety, irritability, or tension. They produce a state of intoxication that is similar to the effect of alcohol and have a high potential for abuse and tolerance development. Depressants have a synergistic effect with alcohol, and this combination is risky. They cause sensory alteration, lessened anxiety, and intoxication. In small amounts they can cause muscle relaxation and calmness, whereas larger amounts can cause slurred speech, impaired judgment, and loss of motor coordination. Large doses of depressants can cause respiratory depression, coma, and even death. Examples of depressants include barbiturates, benzodiazepines, narcotics, and alcohol. Some consider marijuana a depressant.

Stimulants

Stimulants increase alertness and relieve fatigue. Users can feel stronger, more decisive, and euphoric. Some use stimulants to counteract the "down" feeling of depressants or alcohol. Stimulants cause an increase in heart rate and respiratory rate and an elevation in blood pressure. Their effects include dilated pupils and a decreased appetite. High doses of stimulants can cause a rapid or irregular heartbeat, a loss of coordination, perspiration, collapse, blurred vision, dizziness, and feelings of restlessness, anxiety, and delusions. Examples of stimulants include cocaine, amphetamines, and methamphetamine.

Hallucinogens, Marijuana, and Alcohol

Hallucinogens can cause hallucinations, illusions, dizziness, and confusion, along with rapidly changing moods. Large doses can cause convulsions, heart/lung failure, coma, and aneurism. There can sometimes be delayed effects, often called flashbacks, which can occur long after the use of the drug. Chronic use of hallucinogens can cause depression, violent behavior, anxiety, and a distorted perception of time. Examples of hallucinogens include LSD and ecstasy.

Marijuana is derived from cannabis, which is a hemp plant. Effects of marijuana include euphoria soon followed by relaxation, loss of coordination, and increased perception of the senses. Marijuana can impair memory, concentration, and knowledge retention and can cause irritation to the lungs and respiratory system.

Alcohol is the most available and widely used psychoactive substance. Its misuse can represent a difficult diagnostic problem as it is legal to obtain and use. Progression of alcoholism dependence often occurs over an extended period of time. This is unlike some other substances whose progression can be quite rapid. Because of this slow progression, dependence on alcohol can be denied and hidden for long periods of time.

Basic Principles of Learning

Principles of learning, also known as laws of learning, provide additional understanding about what makes people learn most effectively. The first three laws of learning were developed by Edward Thorndike in the early 20th century. They are readiness, exercise, and effect. Five additional principles have joined the first three laws since that time: primacy, recency, intensity, freedom, and requirement.

The principle of readiness includes motivation and concentration. People learn best when they are ready to learn, physically, mentally, and emotionally. Having a strong purpose, a clear objective, and a specific reason for learning something ensures that an individual will make more progress. Also, key to learning is having sufficient rest, health, and physical ability. Learning is an active process and requires that basic needs be met before an individual is capable of learning.

The principle of exercise has to do with repetition, drill, and practice. Students learn best and better retain information with meaningful practice and repetition. Meaningful practice includes positive feedback. The human mind does not usually retain and apply new concepts after a single exposure. Learning continues every time practice occurs. Practice includes recall, review, summary, manual drill, and physical applications, which all serve to create learning habits.

The principle of effect has to do with the emotional reaction that the learner has. It is directly related to motivation. This principle contends that learning is strengthened with pleasant or satisfying feelings, and it is weakened with unpleasant feelings. Positive reinforcement helps motivate learners, and punishment may weaken motivation. Positive feelings accompany feelings of success and of making progress. Believing the task is too difficult may hamper motivation.

The principle of primacy means that the things learned first can create such a strong impression in the mind that they are difficult to erase. Teachers should be careful that that what is taught is right the first time, as unlearning an incorrect first impression is more difficult than learning it correctly the first time. Additionally, a subject matter is best taught in a logical order, step by step, which aids students' learning overall.

The principle of recency asserts that one best remembers the things most recently learned. Alternatively, facts are more difficult to remember the further removed in time the learner is from them. Information that one acquires last is often remembered best, and having important points repeated at the end of a lesson can help cement them in the learner's mind.

The principle of intensity teaches us that the more intense the material taught, the more likely the learner will retain it. Boring learning experiences are not retained as well as dramatic or exciting lessons. Intensity also asserts that a learner will learn more from genuine things than from substitutes or by performing tasks rather than reading about them or seeing them performed. Realism cannot always be achieved in the classroom, but the following can make lessons more intense for the learner: demonstrations, skits, role-playing, examples, analogies, personal experience, and fuller use of the senses (hearing, sight, touch, taste, smell, balance, rhythm, and depth perception).

The principle of freedom asserts that things learned freely and without coercion are better learned. Coercion and compulsion impede learning. Students benefit from freedoms of personal responsibility (freedom of choice, freedom of action, and freedom to bear the results of action) as learning is an active process. Without freedom, students may have little or no interest in learning.

Finally, the law of requirement teaches us that the learner must have something to obtain or do something. The starting point may be an ability, skill, instrument, or anything else that may assist in learning, but a starting point (or root) is necessary.

Classical Conditioning

Through classical conditioning a person can learn a new response or behavior by making associations between previously unrelated things. This type of learning was discovered by Ivan Pavlov, who was a physiologist experimenting with the hunger response of dogs. Pavlov noticed that the dogs he was working with salivated when in the presence of food. The dogs displayed an unconditioned response (salivating) when exposed to the food (the unconditioned stimulus). The unconditioned response is unlearned and occurs naturally (or unconditionally) in response to the unconditioned stimulus. Later, Pavlov paired the food with the sound of a bell. After some time, the dogs would salivate at the sound of the bell, even when it was not paired with food. The bell sound is the conditioned stimulus, and the dog's salivating at its sound is the conditioned response. The conditioned stimulus did not affect the dogs before it was paired with the unconditioned stimulus; after pairing, the dogs display the conditioned response, which is learned and not naturally occurring.

There are three phases to the process outlined here. First is the stage known as before conditioning. This would be the phase when the dogs salivated when exposed to the food. The second stage is during conditioning. This describes the time when the dogs were exposed to the food and bell together. Finally, the last phase is after conditioning. At this time the dogs salivate to the bell alone, without the food.

Fundamental Elements of Classical Conditioning

There are several key phenomena in classical conditioning that behavioral psychologists have described. Some of these are part of attaining the new (conditioned) response, and some have to do with this learned response fading away.

Acquisition describes the learning phase, when the conditioned response is first produced and then increasingly strengthened. For the example used here, a researcher could say that the subject (dog) has acquired the response when it salivates in response to the bell alone. Once the subject has acquired the response, it can be reinforced and strengthened to ensure the subject has learned the response effectively.

Extinction occurs when the learned response (i.e., the conditioned response) either disappears completely or is reduced in strength and/or frequency. Extinction can happen when the conditioned stimulus stops occurring together with the unconditioned stimulus. For Pavlov's dogs, this might occur if they continued to hear the bell without also receiving food. Eventually, the bell would stop causing the salivation response. Without the conditioned response (i.e., salivation) being reinforced at least some of the time with the unconditioned stimulus (i.e., food), the connection between the two weakens or breaks completely.

When a learned response (conditioned response) reappears even after extinction, this is known as spontaneous recovery. If the researchers stop presenting the subject with the conditioned stimulus (i.e., the sound of the bell), they may find that the bell later has no effect or a much decreased effect on the subject. After this has happened, if the conditioned stimulus (bell) is presented and the conditioned response (salivating) occurs, the subject has spontaneously recovered the previously conditioned/learned response. The conditioned stimulus and unconditioned stimulus must be re-associated, or the recovery will not last and extinction will again take place.

When a subject exhibits similar responses to other stimuli that it does to the conditioned stimulus, this is known as stimulus generalization. Examples include dogs that salivate not only to the sound of the bell but also to other similar sounds or a small child who was conditioned to fear a white rat also fearing other fuzzy white objects like stuffed toys.

The ability to differentiate between a conditioned stimulus and other stimuli is stimulus discrimination. Using the examples in the previous paragraph, stimulus discrimination would be seen in the dogs that only salivate to the sound of the bell and not to any other sounds that have not been paired with an unconditioned stimulus, or the child would not fear all fuzzy white objects but only the white rat that was paired with the unconditioned stimulus.

Operant Conditioning

Like classical conditioning, operant conditioning involves behavioral learning affected by outside stimuli. However, classical conditioning involves involuntary reflexes or automatic behaviors (i.e., salivation), and operant conditioning deals with voluntary behaviors. Through operant conditioning, a person makes a connection between a certain behavior and a consequence, either positive or negative.

B. F. Skinner did not believe that classical conditioning was able to adequately explain the complexity of human behavior. Skinner based much of his work on Edward Thorndike's law of effect, which is that behavior that results in satisfying consequences is more likely to be repeated, but behavior that results in unsatisfying or unpleasant consequences is less likely to be repeated. Unlike Thorndike, Skinner was uninterested in studying states of mind or feelings (like satisfaction) and instead developed his framework on things that can be observed, that is, behavior and its consequences.

Skinner added a new concept to the law of effect. Reinforcement is the key to behaviors being strengthened or weakened, according to Skinner. When a behavior is reinforced, it will be repeated, or strengthened; behaviors that are not reinforced will be weakened or even stopped completely.

- 46 -

Skinner referred to the responses, or consequences, of behaviors as operants. Operants are categorized as follows:

> *Neutral*—those that do not strengthen nor weaken a behavior

> *Reinforcers*—those that raise the chances that a behavior will strengthened (repeated), which can be either positive or negative

> *Punishers*—those that lower the chances that a behavior will be strengthened (repeated), which can be positive or negative

Positive reinforcement gives an outcome or consequence that a subject finds pleasant or rewarding. For example, Skinner placed rats in special boxes. If they pressed a certain lever, they would immediately get food.

Negative reinforcement removes an outcome or consequence that a subject does not like. For example, the rat in one of Skinner's boxes could have a loud and unpleasant buzzer going off. The buzzer stops if the rat presses a certain lever.

Positive punishment occurs when an unpleasant stimulus follows a certain behavior; for example, a rat in one of Skinner's boxes could be given a shock when he pushed the "wrong" lever.

Negative punishment involves taking away something positive from the subject, following a certain behavior. For example, a child may have his/her television viewing time taken away if he/she misbehaves.

In positive reinforcement or punishment, something is given to the subject. In negative reinforcement or punishment, something is taken away from the subject. Reinforcement is meant to be pleasant, this is, giving something positive or taking away something negative. Punishment is meant to be unpleasant, that is, giving something negative or taking away something positive. Punishment is often less effective than reinforcement. Often the punished behavior is simply repressed for a time and returns after the punishment no longer occurs.

Schedules of Reinforcement

Behaviorists have learned that not only does the type of reinforcement matter, but when and how often it is delivered matters greatly to how likely it is that a behavior will strengthen or weaken. There are different patterns in which reinforcement can be given. These patterns can be called schedules. Schedules can affect the response rate (i.e., how quickly the subject does the behavior or how hard the subject works) and also the extinction rate (how quickly the subject stops doing the behavior in the absence of reinforcement). Different types of schedules include the following:

> *Continuous reinforcement*—every time a behavior occurs, the subject receives reinforcement. For example, you give your dog a treat every time he/she brings you the ball. With this schedule, the response rate is slow, while the extinction rate is fast.

> *Fixed interval schedule*—after a fixed amount of time since the previous reinforcement, new reinforcement is given as soon as a new correct response is made. For example, you give your dog a treat when he/she brings you the ball after 5 minutes have passed since the last treat. Both response rate and extinction rate are medium for this schedule.

> *Variable interval schedule*—as long as at least one correct response is made, reinforcement comes after a variable (or unpredictable) amount of time goes by. For example, you give

your dog a treat when he/she brings you the ball after varying amounts of time have passed since the last treat. In this schedule the response rate is fast, while extinction rate is slow.

Fixed ratio schedule—reinforcement is given after a certain number of correct responses. For example, you give your dog a treat after he/she brings you the ball five times. Response rate is fast, while extinction rate is medium in this schedule.

Variable ratio schedule—reinforcement is given after an unpredictable number of correct responses. For example, you give your dog a treat at random times after he/she brings you the ball. In this schedule response rate is fast, while extinction rate is slow.

Researchers have found that the variable ratio schedule has the best outcomes for consistent responses and low extinction, although the variable interval schedule also produces a strong outcome. The key appears to be the variable or randomness factor.

Shaping

Skinner developed the process of shaping, a type of behavior modification through operant conditioning. Through shaping, both humans and animals can learn new behaviors, behaviors that do not come naturally to them. An example of shaping is the way that Skinner taught the rats he was working with to press the lever in the Skinner box. Pressing a lever is not something that a rat will do instinctively, so Skinner started by reinforcing behaviors that led the rats closer to the target behavior. This idea of reinforcing behaviors that come closer to the target behavior is referred to as successive approximation. Skinner would first reward the rats when they stepped closer to the lever. Once they did that, he would reward them only for new behaviors, such as stepping even closer, standing on hind legs, and eventually touching the lever. Skinner would not continue to reward previously rewarded behaviors to focus the rats on new behaviors that came closer to the target. Shaping can be used to housetrain dogs, to teach children to do chores, or even to help someone overcome a phobia.

Cognition and Culture in Learning

Situated cognition, or situated learning, is the theory that a person's knowledge is rooted in the context, culture, and activity in which it was learned. As people learn while interacting with each other and through language and shared ideas, learning is social and not isolated. Learning occurs as people discuss, share knowledge, and solve problems together. A form of socio-cultural learning is cognitive apprenticeship in which an expert shares important skills, interactions, and experiences with a novice learner. This theory has helped researchers better understand how people learn as it focuses on what people learn in their everyday lives, which are authentic contexts for a variety of skills. The theory also helps educators understand how to build on knowledge and skills that their students may already possess.

Albert Bandura asserted that the world (environment) and a person's behavior cause or influence each other. He called this reciprocal determinism. This contrasts with behaviorism's assertion that one's environment causes one's behavior. See the previous section on Albert Bandura and his social learning theory for more on this topic.

Environmental and Cultural Influences on Learning

Some factors that influence the process of learning include relationships, stress, and physical health. The more positive the relationship between student and teacher, whether in a formal or informal setting, the better the student will learn and make connections between old and new knowledge. A certain level of stress can be beneficial to learning as adrenaline can stimulate the brain. Chronically stressful environments have a negative influence on learners. Students who live in chronically stressful environments tend to have lower levels of immunity, aptitude, concentration, and comprehension skills. Physical health factors that influence learning include being sufficiently rested, having sufficient physical activity during one's day, and nutrition.

Culture can also influence learning style. People from some cultures prefer verbal instructions, whereas those from other cultures may prefer visual or written instructions. Still others learn best by observing and then doing.

Some cultures emphasize hierarchy. In these cultures, teachers are often seen as the experts, and students are expected to respect them and expect that they will give them the information they need. In such cultures debate and discussion can be seen as a lack of respect for the teacher. Other cultures are more egalitarian, and teachers serve as facilitators and expect debate and discussion from their students.

Another cultural distinction is between individualism and communitarianism. Western countries, and by extension their educational systems, are generally individualistic. Students are expected to be as independent as possible, and teachers provide only essential information and guidance for them to get started on their assignments. In most Western contexts, students are expected to work independently and not collaborate with other students, which can be seen as copying others' work or ideas. Other cultures, for example, most Asian cultures along with others, are more community oriented. In communitarian cultures, group collaboration is the norm, and teachers may be more accessible and supportive than those found in more individualistic contexts.

There are two main models to explain cultural differences in learning and work settings. The first is Geert Hofstede's cultural dimensions, which he identified to help distinguish one culture from another. He later collaborated with Michael Bond and Michael Minkov to round out the list. Hofstede's dimensions include the following:

- Power distance index (high vs. low)
- Individualism versus collectivism
- Masculinity versus femininity
- Uncertainty avoidance index (high vs. low)
- Pragmatic versus normative
- Indulgence versus restraint

Trompenaars's model of national cultural difference was developed by Fons Trompenaars and Charles Hampden-Turner. It includes five orientations that deal with the ways in which people deal with each other: one that deals with time and one that deals with the environment. Their seven dimensions include the following:

- Universalism versus particularism
- Individualism versus communitarianism
- Specific versus diffuse
- Neutral versus emotional
- Achievement versus ascription
- Sequential time versus synchronous time
- Internal direction versus outer direction

Memory Encoding

Information that enters a person's memory system from sensory input must be changed into a form that the system can cope with to store it. The three primary ways that information can be changed or encoded include the following:

- Visual
- Acoustic
- Semantic (meaning)

There is evidence to suggest that the principal coding system in short-term memory (STM) is acoustic coding. People often try to hold a long list of new information, such as a list of numbers or names, by verbally rehearsing them. The principal encoding system in long-term memory (LTM) is likely semantic coding (i.e., by meaning). Information in LTM can be coded both acoustically and visually. STM is also referred to as working memory.

Effortful processing describes learning or storing/encoding information that requires attention and effort. This is used when one requires practice and rehearsal to remember something. When any type of technique is utilized to better remember information, one is engaged in effortful processing.

Automatic processing describes a situation in which an activity can be completed successfully without any thought. Often this is something that has been completed many times before and can also be referred to as muscle memory.

Memory Storage

The term *memory storage* describes where information is stored, the duration of the storage, the capacity for storage, and what kind of information is being stored. The way that information is stored affects the way it is retrieved, and there is a considerable amount of research about the differences between short-term memory (STM) and long-term memory (LTM).

A normal adult has between five and nine slots for items in STM. The amount of information can be expanded greatly depending on how much information one can "chunk" together in each of the slots. This contrasts with the capacity of LTM, which is believed to be unlimited. Information in STM is stored for a brief period of time, between 0 and 30 seconds, whereas LTM can last an entire lifetime.

For memories to pass from STM to LTM memory, they must go through stabilization, which allows the memory to become resistant to interference from competing stimuli or disrupting factors. Stabilization requires the passage of time and leads to consolidation, or short-term memories finding a permanent place in LTM. Physiologically establishing long-term memories involves physical changes in the structure of neurons in the brain. This is known as long-term potentiation. At the most basic level, when something is learned, circuits of neurons in the brain called neural networks are created, altered, or strengthened. These neural networks are made up of neurons that communicate through special junctions called synapses. With repeated use, the strength of these circuits of neurons is reinforced. This reinforcement facilitates the passage of nerve impulses and may involve connections to the visual cortex, the auditory cortex, or other associative regions of the cortex.

Short-term memories are sustained by neural networks in the frontal, prefrontal, and parietal lobes of the brain. Long-term memories are supported and maintained by more stable and permanent changes in neural networks spread widely throughout the brain. The hippocampus serves as a type of temporary transit point for long-term memories, although it is not itself used to store information. The hippocampus is essential to the process of consolidation of information from STM to LTM. Additionally, it is believed to be involved in modifying neural connections for 3 months or more after the initial learning of the information.

Memory Retrieval

Memory retrieval refers to accessing the information that is in storage. When one is unable to remember something, the issue may be that he/she is unable to retrieve it. In retrieval, the differences between STM and LTM are clear. In STM items are stored and retrieved sequentially, whereas in LTM items are stored and retrieved by association. Organization, such as sequencing, can help aid retrieval.

Forgetting in LTM can be explained by interference. The theory of interference proposes that information that is similar in format sometimes gets in the way of the information that one is attempting to recall. The two types of interference are retroactive and proactive. Retroactive interference describes a situation in which more recent information gets in the way of trying to recall older information. Proactive interference is the reverse; old information prevents the recall of new information.

The so-called tip-of-the-tongue phenomenon describes difficulty retrieving information from LTM. Usually this is a commonplace or well-known piece of information such as someone's name, and may feel just out of reach. A retrieval cue can be helpful in retrieving this type of information. A retrieval cue is a type of stimulus to help one remember the information one is trying to retrieve. This can include information about where one was when he/she learned the information; what other people were there; what the topics of conversation were; what tastes, sounds, or smells were present; or even what mood someone was in.

Context dependency in memory has to do with the phenomenon of the added ease of memory retrieval when the context (i.e., circumstances around the memory) is the same for both the original encoding and the retrieval. Research has shown improvement in recall of specific information when these two contexts match. An example of this is seen when someone returns to a childhood home and is able to more readily remember events that occurred. A practical use for this phenomenon is to physically reenact an event to remember some details, such as retracing one's steps after misplacing an item.

At times, a person will add in details to a memory that did not actually occur. This is referred to as constructive memory. Constructive memory describes using knowledge to organize new information and fill in gaps. Human memory is not an unvarnished duplicate of the past but rather relies on constructive processes. These sometimes have a tendency to have errors and distortions.

Sensory Memory

Sensory memory describes the ability to retain the impression of sensory information for a brief time after the original stimuli have ended. It is the shortest-term element of memory and allows a person to remember great sensory detail about a complex stimulus just after its presentation. Sensory memory is an automatic response and is thought to be outside of cognitive control. No manipulation of the incoming information occurs in sensory memory as it is transferred quickly to working memory. During this transfer, the amount of information is greatly reduced due to the lack of capacity of working memory to handle all the input from our sensory organs.

It is thought that there is a subtype of sensory memory for each of the five major senses: touch, taste, sight, hearing, and smell. Only three of these types have been studied extensively: those of echoic memory (auditory), iconic memory (visual), and haptic memory (touch).

Iconic memory, named for the mental representations of visual stimuli (icons), has a duration of about 100 milliseconds and fades quickly. Echoic memory (auditory system) can hold information for a bit longer, about 3 to 4 seconds. Haptic memory holds memories of sensations all over the body before these either vanish or are transported into STM and seems to last about 2 seconds.

Implicit and Explicit Memory

Implicit memory, or non-declarative memory, is a long-term memory function and includes motor skills, cognition, and learning. Implicit memory is also known as procedural memory. In contrast, explicit memory, or declarative memory, deals with how one knows something and includes general knowledge and events that an individual has personally experienced.

Mnemonic Devices

Mnemonic devices are tools or techniques that one can use to remember something better. They are shortcuts that help a person associate the facts or information one wants to remember with an image, a sentence, or a word. These techniques are common and date back to ancient Greek times. Much of the time, one may be using a mnemonic device without even knowing it. Mnemonic devices are a way of memorizing information so that it stays in the brain longer and can be more easily recalled.

The following are types of mnemonic devices:

- *Music mnemonics*—use of songs or jingles, such as singing the ABCs
- *Name mnemonics*—combining the first letter of each word into a new word, such as ROY G BIV for the colors of the rainbow
- *Expression or word mnemonics*—combining the first letter of each word to form a phrase or sentence—Kings Play Chess On Funny Green Squares for the classifications of living organisms (Kingdom, Phylum, etc.)
- *Model mnemonics*—using a model, such as a pyramid or chart
- *Ode mnemonics*—using a poem or doggerel, such as "Thirty days hath September, April, June, and November"
- *Note organization mnemonics*—such as notecards, outlines, or the Cornell system (main ideas or questions to the left of a vertical line with details or answers to the right)
- *Image mnemonics*—constructed in the form of a picture, often the sillier the better, such as a picture of a sick bat for the depressant drugs (i.e., barbiturates, alcohol, or tranquilizers)
- *Connection mnemonics*—new knowledge connected to previously learned knowledge. For example, it's easy to remember the direction of longitude and latitude because longitude has an N it in, which stands for north, so longitude must run north-south. As latitude has no N, it must run east-west.
- *Spelling mnemonics*—for example, the principal at school is your pal, and a principle is a rule
- *Method of loci*—also called the memory palace. This method takes a place and assigns items to memorize with all the objects in the place. An example is using one's own home, and the rooms and furniture become the objects of information. Another example is the route one takes to work, with the landmarks standing for the information to be memorized.

Elaborative Rehearsal and Levels of Processing

Elaborative rehearsal is another memory technique; it entails contemplating the meaning of the term or idea to be remembered rather than simply repeating it to oneself over and over. It can be used to relate two concepts to one another to give them meaning or relating new knowledge to older knowledge.

The levels of processing model concentrates on the depth of processing involved in memory. This model predicts that the deeper the information is processed, the longer the memory will last. Depth refers to the meaningfulness taken from the exercise rather than how much the material is analyzed. This model comes from the basic idea that memory is what happens as a result of processing information. According to this approach, there are three ways to process information: structural processing and phonemic processing, which both are called shallow processing, or semantic processing, which is referred to as deep processing.

Structural processing is based on appearance and occurs when one encodes the physical qualities of something, such as the typeface of a word or how the letters look. Phonemic processing occurs when one encodes the sound of ideas or information. As both of these (structural and phonemic processing) are shallow processing, they involve only maintenance of information and lead to fairly short retention of the material.

Semantic processing is also considered deep processing and happens when one encodes the meaning of a word and relates it to similar words with similar meaning. Deep processing involves elaborate rehearsal and a more meaningful analysis of information. This leads to better recall.

Concepts and Prototypes

A concept is a mental grouping of similar items; it is used to better remember and understand what things are, their meaning, and what categories or groups they are part of. Concepts can be used for generalizing information, making associations and discriminations, speeding up memory, and guiding actions and behaviors.

A prototype is the best example or central member of a category. Prototypes can be used to enhance memory and recall as one can compare newer, similar items to the prototype to categorize, identify, or store the new item.

Schema

A schema is a way of organizing information about the world, a framework for understanding complex ideas. For example, a child may have a schema for dog—hair-covered animal with four legs and a tail. When he/she first sees a horse, he/she may erroneously call it a dog because it fits with the schema (i.e., hair covered with four legs and a tail). When he/she is corrected and learns that this is a different animal, he/she will then have a schema for horse, which is a bigger animal than a dog that also has hooves.

People have many types of schemata to help understand the world. Some may help one know how to behave in unfamiliar social situations; others may help one understand what new objects are. Schemata have been called the building blocks of a mental model for the world and how it works. People learn new information much more quickly when they can fit it into an existing schema—this is called assimilation. When new information does not fit into an existing schema, the person must either change the existing schema or create a new one—called accommodation. Many times, it is difficult for people, especially adults, to make these changes, and they instead ignore new

- 53 -

information or distort it in their minds so that it fits with their worldview. An example of this is prejudice or stereotypes. These can be difficult to change, and people often ignore or create alternate explanations for compelling information that is contrary to their existing schemata.

Mental Set and Functional Fixedness

A mental set is a framework for thinking about a problem, shaped by habit or desire. A mental set can make it easy to solve a type of problem, but if one attaches to the wrong mental set, problem-solving and creativity is inhibited. Another way to think about mental sets is as subconscious tendencies to approach a problem in a particular way. Past experiences and habits shape them. An inappropriate mental set can obstruct the solution of otherwise straightforward problems. An example of this is the question, "When a U.S. plane carrying Canadian passengers crashes in international waters, where should the survivors be buried?" The wording implies that this is a problem of international law (a mental set), when the fact is that survivors would not need to be buried.

One form of mental set is functional fixedness, which is a cognitive bias that limits a person to use an object or tool only in the way it is traditionally used. One example of this is someone who needs a weight but fails to use an available hammer because his/her mental set is to think of the hammer as for a specific purpose only and nothing else. Functional fixedness has been called a mental block against using an item in a new way to solve a problem.

Algorithms

An algorithm is a defined set of step-by-step procedures that will provide the correct answer to a particular problem. Often thought of as a purely mathematical term, one can follow the same type of process to guarantee finding the correct answer when problem-solving or decision-making. Step-by step approaches can be useful when each decision must be made following the same process and when accuracy is essential. A possible downside to using an algorithm to solve a problem is that the process tends to be time-consuming and may not work when decisions need to be made quickly. With algorithms, accuracy is increased and potential mistakes are minimized, but decisions cannot be made swiftly.

Heuristics

A heuristic is a mental shortcut that allows a person to make judgments and solve problems quickly. Heuristics are usually informed by one's past experiences and allow a person to act without delay. However, heuristics don't always guarantee a correct solution. Mistakes may occur, but heuristics allow for speedy decisions when time is of the essence. An example of a heuristic in everyday life is in deciding the best route to get from point A to point B. It would be most efficient to use a route that one knows has worked well in the past. An algorithm approach to this problem would entail mapping out every possible route to determine which one would be fastest, but this would be a time-consuming process. Heuristics can be helpful, but they can also lead to cognitive biases. They can speed up the decision-making process, but they can also introduce errors. Simply because something worked in the past does not mean it will work again. Relying on heuristics can make it difficult to see alternative solutions or come up with new ideas. They can also contribute to stereotypes and prejudice. As these mental shortcuts can be used to classify and categorize people, one can often overlook more relevant information.

Types of heuristics include the availability heuristic, the anchoring heuristic, and the representativeness heuristic

Availability Heuristic

This strategy involves making decisions simply based on how easy it is to bring something to mind. One may remember most quickly a number of examples relevant to the decision or problem. As these are most readily available in the memory, one is likely to judge them as being more common or frequently occurring than they actually are. An example is thinking of recent plane crashes and thus believing that it is safer to travel by car. Simply because the examples of air disasters came to mind so easily, the availability heuristic leads one to think that plane crashes are more common than they actually are.

Representativeness Heuristic

This strategy involves making a decision by comparing one's present situation to the more representative mental prototype. For example, if trying to determine another person's trustworthiness, one might compare aspects of the individual in question to other mental examples one holds. A sweet older man may remind a person of his/her grandfather, and he/she might assume the person is kind and trustworthy. If you meet someone who is into aromatherapy, yoga, and spiritual healing, you might assume that person is a holistic healer or yoga teacher rather than a scientist or teacher.

Anchoring Heuristic

Also called focalism, this can be thought of as the first impression heuristic. This heuristic describes the tendency to rely too heavily on the first piece of information (which serves as the anchor) when making decisions. This gives the anchoring piece of information a great deal of influence over future assessments.

Confirmation Bias

Confirmation bias is the tendency to interpret new evidence as confirmation of one's existing beliefs or theories. It involves favoring information that confirms previously held beliefs and discounting information that does not support them. It impacts how people gather, interpret, and recall information. When a person supports or opposes a particular issue, he/she may seek only information that supports his/her beliefs and also interprets news stories in a way that upholds his/her ideas.

Hindsight Bias

Hindsight bias is also known as creeping determinism or the knew-it-all-along effect. It is the inclination, after an event has occurred, to see the event as having been predictable, despite there having been little or no objective basis for this prediction. Hindsight bias can cause memory distortion and can also lead to extreme methodological problems when trying to understand and interpret results of experimental studies. There are three levels of hindsight bias that "stack" on each other and compound the issue. The first level is memory distortion, such as misremembering an earlier opinion or judgment (i.e., "I said it would happen"). The second level is inevitability and centers on our belief that the event was inevitable (i.e., "It had to happen"). The third level is foreseeability and involves the belief that we personally could have foreseen the event (i.e., "I knew it would happen").

Theories of Personality

There are four major approaches to personality theories: trait, psychoanalytic, humanistic, and social-cognitive.

Psychoanalytic Approach to Personality

The psychoanalytic perspective of personality was created by Sigmund Freud and emphasizes the unconscious mind and the importance of early childhood experiences. Freud asserted that dreams, free association, and slips of the tongue could reveal things hidden in the unconscious. Other theorists who follow the psychoanalytic perspective agreed with Freud about the importance of the unconscious but disagreed with other parts of his theories. These Neo-Freudian theorists include Erik Erikson, Carl Jung, Alfred Adler, and Karen Horney. Erikson emphasized how personality is shaped over the course of the entire life span, the social elements of personality development, and the identity crisis. Jung concentrated on ideas like psychological types, the collective unconscious, and archetypes. Adler asserted that the desire to achieve superiority is the core motive behind personality and that this stems from primal and universal feelings of inferiority. Horney's work emphasized the societal and cultural factors that play roles in personality including the significance of the parent-child relationship. She focused on the need to overcome a sense of isolation and basic anxiety.

The Humanistic Perspective on Personality

This approach emphasizes psychological growth, personal awareness, and free will. Its outlook on human nature is more positive than some other approaches. It focuses on how each individual can achieve his/her potential. Two major humanistic theorists are Carl Rogers and Abraham Maslow. Rogers focused on the importance of free will and psychological growth and believed in the goodness of people. Rogers asserted that the driving force behind human behavior is the actualizing tendency. Maslow theorized that people are motivated by a hierarchy of needs, with the most basic needs being those necessary for life (food, water, and shelter). Maslow asserted that as people move up in the hierarchy as the more basic needs are met, they can then focus on things such as love, belonging, and even self-actualization.

Trait Perspective of Personality

The trait perspective centers on identifying, measuring, and describing the specific traits that make up human personality. Researchers believe they can better comprehend the differences among individuals through understanding these traits. Major theorists of the trait perspective include Hans Eysenck Raymond Cattell, Robert McCrae, and Paul Costa. Eysenck asserted that there are three dimensions of personality: extraversion-introversion, emotional stability-neuroticism, and psychoticism. Cattell recognized 16 personality traits that he asserted could be used to understand and measure individual differences in personality. McCrae and Costa identified five key dimensions of personality in their big five theory. These dimensions are extraversion, neuroticism, openness to experience, conscientiousness, and agreeableness.

Social Cognitive Perspective on Personality

The social cognitive perspective emphasizes the importance of self-efficacy, cognitive processes, observational learning, and situational influences. The primary theorist is Albert Bandura, who promoted the importance of learning through observation or social learning. Bandura's theory highlighted the role of conscious thoughts, including our own beliefs in our abilities, or self-efficacy.

Personality Assessment Tools

Personality assessment tools, also called personality tests by the layperson, can be used both to help diagnose psychological problems as well as assess people applying for jobs or colleges or who are involved with the court system. These tools generally fall into two different categories: self-report assessments and projective assessments. Self-report assessments have the participant choose from set options. These can be true/false, a Likert scale (rating from strongly agree to strongly disagree), or multiple choice. Projective assessments require the participant to produce a response to an ambiguous prompt, such as a picture or an incomplete sentence. Projective assessments require much more input from the evaluator and often rely on the evaluator's interpretation of the participant's responses.

The Minnesota Multiphasic Personality Inventory (MMPI) is perhaps the most widely utilized assessment that assesses multiple dimensions of personality. A self-report assessment, it uses true/false questions and takes 1 to 2 hours to complete. The MMPI was originally developed to measure psychopathology. The first MMPI was published in 1942. The MMPI-2 is the updated version that came out in 1989; there is also a shorter version, the MMPI-2-RF, which takes about half the time to complete. It is now used widely in not only therapeutic assessment but also in screening candidates for jobs and for college and career counseling. The domains that the MMPI assesses are hypochondriasis, depression, hysteria, psychopathy, masculinity versus femininity, paranoia, psychasthenia, schizophrenia, hypomania, and social introversion. The MMPI can also be used to assess the big five personality traits (i.e., aggressiveness, psychoticism, disconstraint, neuroticism, and introversion).

An example of a projective assessment is the Rorschach Inkblot Test, created by 1921 by Hermann Rorschach. The participant is shown images of inkblots and is asked what they see in them. The evaluator can then interpret the participant's response and determine what unconscious feelings or thoughts the participant has revealed. The participant is taken through the inkblots twice and is asked to give a detailed response to explain his/her first impression of each one. The Rorschach test has been found to be useful to measure anxiety, psychosis, and depression. Evaluators for the Rorschach test must have proper training and experience to correctly interpret test results. The scoring system that has been developed for the Rorschach test is the Exner scoring system and is used to code the participant's responses for the following characteristics:

- Form
- Movement
- Chromatic color
- Achromatic color
- Shading-texture
- Shading-dimension
- Shading-diffuse
- Form dimension
- Pairs and reflections

A similar test is the Thematic Apperception Test (TAT), developed by Henry Murray and Christiana Morgan in the 1930s. The participant taking the TAT is shown eight to 12 pictures and is asked to tell a story about each one. The pictures are ambiguous and can be interpreted many ways. The evaluator gleans insight into the participant through the stories that the participant tells. The participant reveals interests, hopes, fears, and goals in the stories. Both the Rorschach and the TAT tests rely on the professional judgment of the evaluators, but the TAT test does not have a formal scoring system like the Exner system of the Rorschach.

Attribution

Attribution in social psychology is how individuals attach meaning to others' behavior or their own. It is the process through which a person explains the causes of behavior and events. One way to categorize the types of attribution is internal versus external. In internal attribution, or personal attribution, the cause of the behavior in question is credited to the person's characteristics such as personality, efforts, ability, mood, attitudes, or disposition. For external, or situational attributions, the cause of the behavior in question is credited to the situation in which the behavior was seen (e.g., task, other people, or luck). In other words, external attribution proposes that the individual produces the behavior because of the surrounding environment or social situation, whereas internal attribution proposes that a person's behavior is due to his/her own characteristics. These two attribution types cause different perceptions of the person engaging in a behavior.

When people seek to find rationale for behaviors, they are likely to become ensnared with biases and errors. Some examples of such attributional biases follow.

Fundamental Attribution Error and Self-Serving Bias

The fundamental attribution error is most noticeable when people explain and assume others' behavior. It is the habit to explain a person's behavior based on internal factors (such as character or intention) and disregard external factors (such as situational influences). It is more common for a person to exaggerate the influence of internal factors on others' behavior and ignore the situational context. In contrast, when evaluating one's own behavior, it is more common for a person to exaggerate situational factors when there is a negative outcome and dispositional factors when there is a positive outcome. This is also known as self-serving bias.

Dispositional Attribution

Dispositional attribution describes a person's tendency to attribute people's behavior to internal factors, such as personality, character, and ability. For example, when encountering a rude worker, a customer may decide that the worker is simply a bad person, not taking into account all the events and factors that may have led to the worker being rude in that moment. Dispositional attribution is attributing the worker's behavior to his/her personality instead of considering situational factors that may have contributed.

Cultural Bias

Cultural bias occurs when someone makes an assumption about the actions of another based on his/her own cultural beliefs and practices. People from individualist cultures, such as those of Anglo-Saxon European descent, generally value individuals' personal goals and independence, whereas those from collectivist cultures emphasize membership in families, tribes, nations, and other groups over individuality. Collectivist cultures value conformity and interdependence more than independence. The type of culture a person comes from (individualist or collectivist) affects how one makes attributions. People from individualist cultures are more likely to make fundamental attribution errors (attributing someone's behavior on internal factors), whereas collectivist cultures tend to attribute a person's behavior more to external factors. Also, those from individualist cultures utilize self-serving bias more than collectivist cultures. This is the tendency to attribute success to internal factors and failure to external factors. The reverse is typical of those from collectivist cultures. Called the self-effacing bias, a person is more likely to attribute success to externalities and failure on internalities (the individual).

Just-World Hypothesis

The just-world hypothesis is an example of defensive attribution, which refers to a set of beliefs an individual holds to defend his/herself from concerns that he or she will be the cause or victim of some misfortune. In the just-world hypothesis, good things happen to good people, and bad things happen to bad people. This perspective helps people avoid feeling vulnerable to situations over which they have no control. It can lead to victim blaming, even in catastrophic situations. For example, after a car accident, others may conclude that a person was at fault, even when little information is available. This allows them to believe it is something that they will not "allow" to happen to them.

Actor/Observer Difference

Individuals are more likely to attribute the behavior of other people to their dispositional factors and their own behavior to situational factors. The same behavior can be attributed differently depending on the person's role—as actor or observer. When individuals observe other people (especially those they do not know well), they are more likely to focus on the person, whereas when the same individuals are actors, they tend to focus on situational factors. An example is scoring poorly on a test. An individual is more likely to attribute his/her own poor score to situational factors (e.g., lack of sleep, illness, or teacher asking about material not covered in class) but is more likely to attribute others' poor scores to internal factors (laziness or inattentiveness).

Cognitive Dissonance

Cognitive dissonance is the psychological stress or mental discomfort a person experiences when he/she simultaneously holds contradictory beliefs, values, or ideas. Cognitive dissonance occurs when a person performs an action that contradicts his/her personal beliefs, values, and ideals or when he/she is confronted with new information that contradicts these same beliefs, values, and ideals. The level of dissonance experienced depends on factors including how highly a belief is valued and how much the beliefs/behaviors are inconsistent. More personal beliefs and the importance of the beliefs tend to result in greater dissonance. The greater that the dissonance is, the more pressure the individual will feel to relieve the feelings of discomfort. The three key ways to reduce cognitive dissonance are as follows:

- Focus on more supportive beliefs that outweigh the dissonant belief or behavior. For example, a person who works sitting at a desk all day learns that sitting for long periods of time is linked to a shortened life span. He/she may seek out other information that disputes this link.
- Reduce the importance of a conflicting belief. In the same example as described, the person may justify his/her behavior (prolonged sitting) by believing that other healthy behaviors make up for his/her sedentary lifestyle.
- Change the conflicting belief so that it is consistent with other beliefs or behaviors. This can be the most difficult strategy, particularly in the case of deeply held values.

Attitude

Attitude means a set of beliefs, behaviors, and emotions toward something or someone. Attitudes are enduring (although change is possible) and are often the result of upbringing or experience. They have a powerful influence over one's behavior. An attitude is a learned tendency to evaluate things in a certain way. The components that make up attitudes include the affective, the behavioral, and the cognitive. They can be explicit or implicit—conscious or unconscious—but they all affect our beliefs and behavior.

Attitudes can change through the same influences that lead to their formation. Classical conditioning, operant conditioning, and observational learning can all form or change one's attitudes. Cognitive dissonance (see pervious section) can also lead to change in attitude. People make changes to reduce the discomfort coming from incompatible beliefs. People can also be persuaded to change their attitudes both through message and messengers. Messages can appeal to one's logic or emotions. The characteristics of the person bringing the message can also lead to a shift in attitude, although this tends to be more temporary.

Stereotypes, Prejudice, and Discrimination

Prejudice is an unjustified or incorrect attitude toward an individual based solely on the individual's membership of a group (e.g., race, sex, national origin, religion, etc.). Discrimination involves actions that occur when this attitude is acted upon. An example of discrimination is different standards (consciously or unconsciously) for male and female students. Stereotypes are fixed, overgeneralized beliefs about a group or class of people. Stereotypes are a way that people simplify the world; they reduce the amount of processing (thinking) necessary when meeting a new person. Stereotyping leads one to infer a whole range of abilities and characteristics that one assumes all members of a certain group have.

Group Dynamics

The study of how different groups interact with each other and how individuals behave in groups is called group dynamics. Group dynamics looks at the processes of groups, including membership, influence, conflict, communication, leadership, and teamwork. In addition, group dynamics also examines how groups change over time and how individual people change within groups. Group dynamics are essential to understanding social prejudice and discrimination. The three primary components that affect how well a group works together are personal factors, leadership factors, and environmental factors.

Groupthink

Irving Janis formulated the groupthink model in the early 1970s. Groupthink occurs in groups of people and is a phenomenon in which the need for conformity in the group leads to dysfunctional or irrational decision-making. According to Janis, the eight symptoms of groupthink are the following:

- Illusions of invulnerability leads to overly optimistic risk taking.
- Unquestioned beliefs result in ignoring of consequences and possible moral problems.
- Rationalizing keeps members from re-evaluating their beliefs and can cause them to ignore warning signs.
- Stereotyping leads to ignoring or demonizing those who oppose or challenge the group's ideas.
- Self-censorship causes members who have doubts to hide their fears or misgivings.
- Mindguards are members or leaders who hide problematic information from the group.
- Illusions of unanimity are the belief that everyone is in agreement.
- Direct pressure to conform leads to those who question the group to being seen as disloyal.

Conformity

Conformity describes the tendency that people have to match their speech and actions to that of those around them. People can conform due to either overt social pressure or to unconscious influence of the group. There are many factors that influence the likelihood of conformity including size of the group, how clear or ambiguous the situation is, whether a person comes from an individualistic culture or a collectivist culture, how difficult a task is, how important a task is, and individual personality differences. As people grow older, they are less likely to conform, although we see conformity at all ages.

Sometimes people outwardly conform to the group but privately disagree. This is called compliance and is motivated by a desire for approval by the group. Identification describes a situation in which a person conforms to someone he/she respects and admires. Identification reflects a deeper conformity than compliance. The deepest form of conformity is internalization. Internalization occurs when the individual takes on the group's beliefs as his/her own; there is no difference between the public performance of the norm and the individual's private thoughts.

There are different types of conformity. A desire to fit in with the group and avoid rejection leads to normative conformity. This may lead to a weaker conformity (i.e., compliance) with the individual privately opposing the views of the group. Informational conformity stems from an individual's lack of knowledge and desire for guidance from the group. Informational conformity often leads to internalization, which is a stronger form of conformity.

Deindividuation

Deindividuation is the loss of self-awareness in groups. It occurs when a person loses his/her sense of individual identity. An example can be seen when a person who normally refrains from aggression displays aggressive behavior in an aggressive crowd. People in crowds can feel anonymous and have lessened awareness of individuality. This can reduce their sense of guilt and fear of punishment. This increases with the size of the crowd. Another example is that warriors who disguise their appearance (e.g., through face paint) tend to be more aggressive. Aggression in crowds can be reduced when there are obvious CCTV cameras at crowded events (such as sporting events). Deindividuation can also lead to pro-social behavior, for example, in religious gatherings. Not all people are negatively (or positively) affected by crowds as deindividuation does not affect everyone the same way.

Diffusion of Responsibility

Researchers have found that individuals are less inclined to act or intervene when they are with a large group. If someone has a medical issue on a sidewalk and obviously needs help, those around will be less likely to help if there is a large crowd of people there versus if there are just one or two. This may seem counterintuitive, but due to the presence of so many others, no single person feels compelled to respond—the feeling of responsibility has been diffused among all of the people in the crowd. Diffusion of responsibility causes the bystander effect described previously (the greater number of people present, the less likely anyone will help someone who needs it).

When bystanders actually know the person in distress, they are more likely to help. Bystanders are less likely to help in an ambiguous situation—if they are unsure about what is happening, if the person really needs help, or what should be done. If the distressed person makes eye contact with someone in the crowd and asks for help, that individual will be more likely to help.

Persuasion

Persuasion is a process through which one tries to convince others, without coercion, to change the way they think or behave. Persuasion takes place through straightforward methods and also through manipulation and deceit. Techniques can appeal to either one's logic or emotions. Robert Cialdini describes six different types of persuasion, which he calls weapons of influence. These "weapons" are as follows:

- *Reciprocity*—wanting to return a favor that has been done for you
- *Commitment/consistency*—the idea that people are more likely to follow through when they have committed to something
- *Social proof*—seeing others do something leading one to being willing to do it him/herself
- *Authority*—people trusting those they see as being knowledgeable and trustworthy
- *Liking*—people being more likely to be persuaded by someone they like
- *Scarcity*—limited availability making things more desirable

Methods of persuasion include the following:

- *Foot in the door*—people often feel obligated to comply with bigger requests if they first comply with a small request. The smaller request serves as an opening to the persuader.
- *Door in the face*—this is the opposite of the foot-in-the-door technique. The persuader makes a large request that is denied. The persuader then makes a much smaller request that is now more likely to be granted.
- *Ingratiation*—the persuader tries to acquire the approval of the other person, which makes them more likely to grant a request. Flattery is a form of ingratiation, as are opinion conformity (revising one's opinion to match the other person's) and self-presentation (presenting oneself in a pleasing way).
- *Low ball*—this is changing the price at the last moment from a lower price to a higher one. One may be more likely to go along with the change if it seems an agreement was already reached.
- *Norm of reciprocity*—if the persuader has already done something for the other person, he/she is more likely to comply with the persuader's request.

Obedience

Obedience occurs when one complies with a direct order or request, as opposed to conformity, which occurs through social pressure. The individual giving the order to be obeyed generally has some authority or a higher social status. Conformity relates to one's relationship to peers and the desire for social acceptance.

In the 1950s psychologist Stanley Milgram set up experiments to determine how obedient to authority most people are. Milgram was inspired by the trial of the Nazi Adolf Eichmann, who claimed he was only following orders and felt no guilt for his actions as he was only doing what his superiors requested. Milgram wanted to find out how far most people would go under the pressure to obey. Milgram placed participants in a room and instructed them to deliver electrical shocks to another person in another room. The person receiving the shocks was a part of the experiment and did not receive shocks but acted out the responses to the imaginary shocks. Milgram found that 65% of participants were willing to give the highest level of shocks when instructed to by the experimenter.

Following Milgram's experiments, psychologist Philip Zimbardo staged an experiment in the 1970s to study prisoners and prison life. He set up a "prison" and assigned participants in the study to play the roles of either prisoners or prison guards. Zimbardo himself acted as prison warden. The study was meant to last 2 weeks, but Zimbardo discontinued it after only 6 days. The participants had become so involved in their roles, and the guards were using authoritarian techniques to gain the prisoners' obedience. Some guards subjected prisoners to psychological abuse, harassment, and even physical torture. The results of the Stanford Prison experiment demonstrate how easily individuals are influenced by the roles they are asked to play and the situations they are put in.

Interpersonal Relationships

Interpersonal attraction refers to how much people are drawn to one another, either for romantic relationships or friendships. There are multiple factors affecting interpersonal attraction. One is simply proximity, or how physically close one person is to another. It is more likely that a person will form relationships with others who are nearby (i.e., same state, same city, or same part of town) than with those who are farther away. This idea is called the proximity principle. Propinquity is another factor that affects attraction; it refers to how often or how frequently one comes into physical contact with another person (or thing or idea). This frequency leads to increased familiarity with the other, which in turn leads to being more likely to like the other person, thing, or idea. This concept, that the more someone is exposed to something, the more they are attracted to it, is referred to as the mere exposure effect.

Another factor to attraction is similarity. People tend to be attracted more to others who are similar to them in some way. This may be in family background, level of physical attractiveness, political orientation, personal style, values, or manner of communication. People tend to view those like themselves more favorably and those who are different from them more negatively.

Motivation

Motivation is the reason behind a person's actions; it is why someone does what he/she does. Motivation can be either intrinsic or extrinsic. Intrinsic motivation comes from within the person and is focused on a person's interest or enjoyment of the activity and not on rewards or outer pressures. Extrinsic motivation is stimulated by other people or consequences outside of the individual person. A commonplace example of extrinsic motivation is the promise of a reward or the threat of a punishment. Rewards can be an effective way to motivate someone who does not have intrinsic motivation for the task at hand; however, overuse of rewards can lead to even less intrinsic motivation in a process called overjustification. (Research shows that some rewards are more likely to produce this effect than others.) Likewise, threat of punishment can often lead to increased interest in the forbidden activity or object. Because of these challenges with extrinsic motivation, many teachers and leaders wish to increase intrinsic motivation rather than focusing on extrinsic rewards and punishments. Ways to increase intrinsic motivation include an element of challenge in the task, having some control over what activities or tasks one engages in, curiosity about the activity or task, cooperation and competition, and having others recognize one's accomplishments.

Drive Reduction Theory

Clark Hull asserted that all motivation stems from the biological need to maintain homeostasis. Homeostasis is equilibrium: neither too hot nor too cold, neither too hungry nor too full. To maintain homeostasis, the body acts and responds in ways to balance itself. Hull called the tensions that come from an imbalance in homeostasis drives. According to Hull, drives serve as motivation for behavior. A person will seek to reduce any drives; for example, hunger will motivate a person to eat and thirst will motivate a person to drink. Satisfying the drive will then reinforce those behaviors, and the person will be more likely to engage in the same behavior when the drive presents itself in the future (i.e., conditioning).

One criticism of drive reduction theory is that it does not explain behaviors that do not address a drive. Many people eat when they are not hungry, which this theory cannot explain. Additionally, the theory does not adequately address secondary reinforcers and how they affect motivation. Secondary reinforcers do not meet physiological needs. Money is a secondary reinforcer; on its own it does not reduce hunger, but it can be used to purchase food and reduce the hunger drive indirectly. Despite not directly reducing drives, secondary reinforcers are still powerful motivators (e.g., money or pleasurable experiences). Although it later fell out of favor, drive reduction theory had a great influence on how many psychologists viewed motivation. Many later theories either expand on drive reduction theory or present an alternative viewpoint to it.

Incentive Theory

Although drive reduction theory focuses on one's biological needs as motivation for behavior, incentive theory asserts that external rewards are the primary motivation for action. There are some similarities between incentive theory and operant conditioning, in which the subject performs behavior to avoid punishment or to achieve rewards/reinforcement. In the case of incentive theory, however, the desire for the reward comes first, whereas in operant conditioning, the subject learns of the consequence of his/her actions only afterward. Compared to drive reduction theory, incentive theory works in the opposite way. Drive reduction theory posits that the individual seeks to remove an uncomfortable stimulus (e.g., hunger or pain), whereas incentive theory posits that the individual is motivated by a desire to add a positive stimulus.

Another response to drive reduction theory is Maslow's theory of the hierarchy of needs. This is discussed in great detail in a previous section.

Homeostasis

As mentioned in the section on drive reduction theory, homeostasis describes the need of an organism to maintain a certain stability. Homeostasis requires that the organism have a set point (e.g., for temperature, energy level, weight, etc.), an ability to determine if it is or isn't currently at the set point, and physiological and behavioral responses that will help revert to the set point.

Internal and External Cues

Internal, or physiological cues (such as hunger, thirst, or desire) direct us to eat, drink, and pursue sex, but this is only one type of cue. Other cues can also influence a person to eat, even without the physiological signals to do so. External cues can be either sensory or normative. External sensory cues include taste, smell, the way something looks, or even a written description. External normative cues look to consumption norms and expectations of the culture. In our culture, it is expected that people finish the food on their plates, so larger portion sizes can lead to people eating more. In the United States we tend to have larger portion sizes, from candy bars, to soft drinks, to yogurt cartons, which leads to our eating more than our counterparts in other countries. Social cues are another external cue that signals to us that it is time to eat or drink (e.g., eating or drinking with others). Stress also leads people to pursue food or other things without the physiological need for them. Stress tends to change a person's appetite, whether increasing or decreasing it.

In the brain the hypothalamus acts as the link between the neurological system and the endocrine system. When part of the hypothalamus is stimulated a person will feel hunger, thirst, and so on. It also helps the body maintain its set point for weight and sends fewer hunger cues when the body goes above its set point (and likewise sends more hunger cues when the body falls below its set point). The hypothalamus manages these internal cues, but an individual may not pay attention to them and may instead be distracted by external cues for eating or drinking.

Social Motives

The Five Core Social Motives model was developed by Susan Fiske and summarizes social motivations that affect a person's behavior. The five motives are belonging, understanding, controlling, enhancing self, and trusting. According to this system, the root need is belonging, and all others work to facilitate social functioning in groups. Fiske describes the five motives as follows:

> *Belonging*—people are motivated to bond and affiliate with one another

> *Understanding*—to belong, people are motivated to create sufficient shared social understanding

> *Controlling*—people are motivated to feel effective and competitive in both animate and inanimate environments

> *Enhancing self*—people hope that others see them as socially worthy

> *Trusting*—when people view the world as benevolent, they are able to participate in group activities without unnecessary suspicion or vigilance

Theories of Emotion

The James–Lange theory of emotion asserts that the physiological effect comes first and leads to the perception of emotion. Although not working together, both psychologist William James and physiologist Carl Lange, although working separately, proposed that emotions are the result of physical experiences and that the person then interprets the physical experience to determine he/she is feeling an emotion. For example, if a person sees a threat, such as a vicious dog or a bear, he/she will exhibit physiological symptoms—perhaps quickened breath and heartbeat or trembling. The brain then interprets these physical occurrences as the emotion one is feeling—in this case, fear. Expectedly, the James–Lange theory has been met with challenges since it was first asserted. James himself acknowledged that his theory is counterintuitive.

In response to the James–Lange theory, Walter Cannon and Philip Bard developed their own theory of emotion, known as the Cannon–Bard theory or the thalamic theory of emotion. Their theory asserts that the physiological response and the emotional response occur simultaneously; one does not lead to the other. Cannon conducted experiments on the connection between the viscera (internal organs) and emotions. He found that separating the viscera from the central nervous system (by cutting the neural connection) does not change the individual's emotional response. This contradicts the James–Lange theory's assertion that the viscera are responsible for emotions. Cannon also found that the same reactions in the viscera can be seen in both emotional and nonemotional states (such as illness). Finally, Cannon determined that artificially stimulating changes in the viscera (like one would have during an emotional experience) does not produce emotions. The Cannon–Bard theory asserts that both the physiological response and the emotional response are due to the thalamus being stimulated (e.g., from seeing something threatening).

- 65 -

Another theory that seeks to explain the process of emotion relating to physical arousal is the Schachter–Singer Two Factor theory. Stanley Schachter and Jerome Singer asserted that two factors interact and result in an emotion. The theory purports that after experiencing a stimulus, the individual will have a physiological response, which will be cognitively interpreted based on context. A person's past experiences and existing knowledge help form the cognitive interpretations. Schachter and Singer conducted experiments in which they injected subjects with epinephrine (adrenaline). Some subjects were told what side effects they might experience, and others were not. Some subjects were placed with another person who either acted angry or euphoric. Schachter and Singer hypothesized that for the subjects who did not know to expect the side effects of the adrenaline (i.e., arousal), they would seek to explain their physiological state through context and would be more influenced by the person they were with who was in a euphoric or angry state. They found their experiment to support their hypothesis, but there has been later criticism of their theory including that emotions may be experienced before one thinks about them at times.

A final theory of emotion is *the facial feedback hypothesis*. This theory asserts that facial movement can influence emotional experience. The most common example used is that a person who is forced to smile during an unpleasant event will actually find the event more enjoyable. Among the first to suggest that physiological changes can have an impact on an emotion rather than just being the consequence of that emotion was Charles Darwin. He contended that the very expression of an emotion intensifies it and that even the imitation of an emotion can provoke it in one's mind. Later William James wrote, "Refuse to express a passion, and it dies." About a century after Darwin, the facial feedback hypothesis was developed. Modern research primarily focuses on the effects of facial muscular activity. There are two versions of the facial feedback hypothesis. The weak version, which Darwin introduced, is that the physical feedback intensifies or reduces an emotion already present. The strong version of this hypothesis alleges that facial feedback on its own can create the whole emotion.

Role of the Limbic System in Emotions

The entire central nervous system helps control emotions, but the limbic system and autonomic nervous system are especially influential. The limbic system makes up a curved border around the cerebral cortex and the diencephalon. The entire limbic system, which includes the hippocampus, hypothalamus, and amygdala, helps control many emotional, voluntary, endocrine, and visceral responses to the environment. The limbic system is believed to be one of the oldest and most primitive areas of the brain, and similar systems are also found in most other animals, including reptiles. Whereas the limbic system, as a whole, controls what is basically termed *emotions*, the hippocampus helps the brain form and retain memories, which have a central role in learning and development.

There is not 100% consensus regarding which specific brain structures are part of the limbic system. There is much neural overlap among areas of the brain, and so it is difficult to perfectly classify cortical areas. Most scientists consider the limbic system to be made up of the following:

- *Hippocampus*—associated with memory, focus, and motor control
- *Amygdala*—associated with fear and anxious emotions
- *Hypothalamus*—responsible for regulating hormones and maintaining homeostasis
- *Septal nuclei*—connected to pleasure and learning through reinforcement and/or reward
- *Cingulate cortex*—involved with memory and emotion
- Parahippocampal gyrus—helps with memory

- *Mammillary bodies*—connected to the amygdale and hippocampus
- *Fornix*—connects other parts of the brain, including the hippocampus and mammillary bodies

Functions of the limbic system include the following:

- Controlling emotions such as anger and fear
- Regulating eating, hunger, and thirst
- Responding to pleasure and pain
- Controlling the autonomic nervous system (i.e. pulse, blood pressure, breathing, and arousal)
- Sensing sexual satisfaction
- Controlling violent or aggressive behavior
- Responding to sensory information, in particular the sense of smell

Fight-or-Flight Response

Stress is the physiological and psychological response produced when a person experiences something unpleasant or circumstances requiring change and adaptation. Often the person feels strained by the stressor and may even worry that he/she does not have the ability or resources to deal with it.

The fight-or-flight response is also known as hyperarousal or the acute stress response. It is a physiological reaction in response to a perceived threat and is a general discharge of the sympathetic nervous system, which prepares the person or animal for either fighting or fleeing. The physiological changes that occur in the body during the fight-or-flight response are meant to give the body increased speed and strength. There is increased blood flow to the muscles, which is diverted blood flow from other parts of the body. Blood pressure, heart rate, blood sugars, and fats increase to supply the body with extra energy that may be needed. Blood clotting speeds up to prevent excessive blood loss in case of an injury. Increased muscle tension provides extra speed and strength. Physical signs of fight-or-flight that may be apparent to others include rapid heart rate and breathing, pale or flushed skin, dilated pupils, and trembling. After the stressor is gone, it takes the body between 20 and 60 minutes to return to its pre-arousal state. The fight-or-flight response is part of the first stage of general adaptation syndrome.

Selye's General Adaptation Syndrome

Hans Selye's theory describing the stress response among vertebrates is known as the general adaptation syndrome. This model is also called the classic stress response and revolves around the concept of homeostasis. The three stages of general adaptive syndrome are the alarm reaction, the stage of resistance, and the stage of exhaustion.

The alarm reaction occurs when the stressor first appears and the body gathers resources to deal with it. The pituitary gland begins releasing hormones (adrenaline, cortisol, and norepinephrine) into the bloodstream. These hormonal changes increase energy levels and muscle tension, reduce pain sensitivity, slow down the digestive system, and cause blood pressure to rise. In the stage of resistance, the body continues to build up resistance until either the physical resources are depleted or the stressful stimulus is removed. When the body uses up increasing amounts of its resources, the individual becomes increasingly tired and vulnerable to illness. Psychosomatic disorders first begin to appear in the stage of resistance. In the stage of exhaustion, the body is completely drained of resources and the hormones it was using to manage the stressor. The individual will now exhibit behaviors like irritability, avoidance of responsibilities and relationships, anxiety, poor judgment, and self-destructive behavior.

Effect of Stress on Immune System and Cardiovascular Health

The high level of arousal that humans experience when dealing with daily problems and micro-stressors is often unnecessary. Experiencing this level of arousal on a regular basis is associated with many health issues. The constant hormonal upheaval of chronic stress leads to serious health problems like hypertension, diabetes, and heart disease. Ongoing stress is so damaging because, during the stress response, the hormones that get us ready for emergencies also severely depress our immunity and reduce the immune system's ability to fight off antigens. As an example, cortisol decreases inflammation but also decreases white blood cells and NK cells that kill cancer, increases tumor development and growth, and increases the rate of tissue damage and infection. Stress effects are cumulative and build on themselves day by day.

Researchers have found links between stress and headaches, infectious illness, cardiovascular disease, diabetes, asthma, and gastric ulcers. As stress increases the heart rate and raises blood pressure, hypertension becomes more likely. Hypertension is a major risk factor in coronary heart disease. Stress increases blood cholesterol levels through the release of free fatty acids by adrenaline and noradrenaline. Increased cholesterol buildup leads to a raised heart rate. High blood pressure can lead to lesions on artery walls, in which cholesterol tends to get trapped.

Indirectly, stress affects the immune system when individuals use unhealthy coping strategies to deal with stress, such as alcohol or tobacco use, poor diet and lack of exercise due to lack of time, lack of sleep, and others.

Non-Physiological Effects of Stress

Reactions to stress are not only physical but can also be seen in effects on one's cognition, behavior, and emotions. Cognitive signs of stress include mental slowness, confusion, general negativity, persistent worrying, racing thoughts, difficulty concentrating and forgetfulness, and a general sense of overwhelm. Emotional signs of stress include irritability, frustration, overexcitability, feeling overwhelmed and overworked, feeling of helplessness, and apathy. Behavioral indications of stress include a sense of loneliness, decreased sex drive, decreased contact with family and friends, and avoiding others and social isolation.

Without satisfactory methods for handling stress, it can lead to a heightened sense of dysfunction. This can result in increased anxiety or depression, which if they persist for long periods of time, may require professional help to address them. Escalated stress and anxiety without a sufficient coping system are linked to multiple conditions, often accompanied by psychological distress. These include sleepwalking and other sleep disorders, amnesia and other memory problems, generalized anxiety disorder, obsessive-compulsive disorders, phobias, multiple personality, or hypochondriasis.

Sources of Stress

One particular type of stress is role conflict. This occurs when incompatible demands are placed upon a person so that fulfillment of both would be difficult if not impossible. Role conflict occurs when a person tries to respond simultaneously to the demands of different positions one holds (i.e., parent and employee). Role conflict can be experienced for either short or long periods of time and can be situational.

Another significant stressor is caregiver burden. This is an all-encompassing term that describes the physical, financial, and emotional toll of providing care for another person. Caregivers are nonprofessionals who give support and help to family members or others who need regular care. Caregiver burden is a subjective burden; how the caregiver perceives the situation determines the amount of caregiver burden. Four aspects of caregiving that can cause particular strain are having too little time for the caregiver's interests, sadness over the prognosis of the person they are supporting, too much energy being expended for care, and desire for recovery.

Another, more complex source of stress stems from socioeconomic status (SES). This is partly due to the fact that the feeling of lack of control over one's circumstances tends to decline as one descends the socioeconomic ladder. Researchers have found that the more helpless one feels in the face of a given stressor, the more toxic that stressor's effects are. Those with the lowest SES are more than three times as likely to die prematurely as those at the top. For these people depression, heart disease, and diabetes are much more likely as well. This has been called status syndrome, describing the fact that the higher one is in the social hierarchy, the better his/her health is. Even those who experience poverty in childhood, but later attain higher SES, experience consequences of the poverty they experienced into later life. They are more prone to illness and chronic inflammation, which increases the risk of degenerative diseases. Having little to no control over one's circumstances, as those with low SES and more limited resources do, leads to a strain from learned helplessness. Learned helplessness can result from experiencing a fight-or-flight response that continues indefinitely. When this response is activated chronically, it ravages the body.

Strategies for Coping with Stress

Given all the physiological and nonphysiological effects of stress, it is worthwhile to know ways to manage one's stress and reduce its effects. There are multiple strategies that have been proven to reduce the body's stress response, some of which come from the cognitive-behavioral school of thought.

- *Diaphragmatic breathing*—also called deep breathing, this has a physiological effect on the nervous system by activating the hypothalamus, which connects to the pituitary gland, to send neuro-hormones that trigger a relaxation response in the body.
- *Progressive muscle relaxation*—in this exercise, a person alternates between tensing and relaxing different muscle groups throughout the body. A more complete relaxation of muscles is found this way.
- *Self-monitoring*—this is a way to manage stress and anxiety by bringing awareness to one's thoughts and feelings. It involves writing down whenever one has uncomfortable or unpleasant thoughts and feelings, also noting the situation that led up to the feelings and writing out the current emotions one is going through. Some people also rate their feelings on a scale based on how intense the feelings are.
- *Behavioral activation*—this is a strategy that teaches people to be more active in enjoyable and pleasurable areas of life through identifying goals. This increase in activity and connection can help with mood and stress management.
- *Cognitive restructuring*—this cognitive-behavioral coping strategy helps reduce cognitive distortions such as catastrophic thinking.
- *Perceived control*—this is the extent to which a person believes that he/she has control over a situation. It may help reduce stress and offer other health benefits; however, the loss of perceived control or the idea of control being overemphasized can have adverse consequences on health.

Continuity Versus Stages

There has been some debate among developmental psychologists as to whether the process of development occurs smoothly over time or through age-specific periods. This can be referred to as continuity versus stages or continuity versus discontinuity. Some theorists assert that changes in development are just a matter of quantity; children come to display more of certain skills as they develop. Several major theorists outline series of stages in which skills or traits emerge during certain periods of development. Examples of these stages include Erikson's psychosocial development theory or Freud's psychosexual stages.

Critical Periods

Critical periods are time of increased and favored sensitivity to certain aspects of development. For example, the critical period for language occurs in early childhood. Young children are able to acquire languages easily during this time, whereas adults usually struggle to learn a new language.

Stability Versus Change

The issue of stability versus change addresses the question of how much one's personality traits are set and remain stable in expressions throughout a lifetime versus how much these traits can fluctuate throughout the life span. Some theorists assert that personality traits are relatively set in childhood and may become only more pronounced over time. There is evidence that support both sides of this issue. One of the first psychologists to emphasize the importance of early experiences on later development was Freud. He asserted that these early experiences play a formative role in a person's later development.

Human Development

Human development continues throughout the life span; it does not stop once adulthood is reached. The changes seen in babies and children are usually more dramatic and observable, but the progression from young adulthood through middle and late adulthood is no less momentous. The main developmental stages are outlined as follows:

- Infancy takes place from birth through about two years old. During this stage the infant is quite dependent on caregivers for most things; however, there are many psychological characteristics developing. The bond between the infant and caregiver during this stage has great impact on the infant's later emotional development.
- Childhood takes place between the ages of 2 to 10 years old. Throughout childhood, individuals become increasingly independent from their parents and caregivers as they gain more self-control and learn to carry out tasks for themselves. Children's cognitive skills develop throughout this stage in addition to their developing of understanding right and wrong.
- Adolescence takes place between the ages of 10 and 20. Puberty's onset indicates the beginning of adolescence. This stage is dominated by developing one's own identity and seeking independence from parents. Adolescents' thought processes are more logical, complex, and idealistic than those of children.
- Early adulthood takes place between the ages of 20 and 40. Throughout this stage, the individual establishes both personal and financial independence and seeks to consolidate a career. This is also typically the stage in which the individual selects a partner and begins a family.

- Middle age takes place approximately between the ages of 40 and 65. Throughout this stage of life, individuals expand personal and social involvements and responsibilities, advance their careers, and support their offspring in their path to becoming mature individuals.
- Older adulthood takes places from age 65 on. During this stage, the individual must make considerable adjustment to changes in life and self-perception. For many older adults, this stage can be a liberating time when day-to-day responsibilities of caring for children or working have lessened.

Sensation and Perception

The process in which a sensory receptor is stimulated is known as sensation. In this process, nerve impulses travel to the brain. The brain then interprets the impulses as a sound, a visual image, a taste, an odor, touch, or pain. In a process called transduction, the physical stimulus in the environment emits energy that is absorbed by a sensory organ. This causes sensation to occur.

Perception refers to the brain's organization of information it gets from the neural impulses which it then translates and interprets. Perception allows the individual to make sense of the information relayed by the physical stimulus. When the brain processes information to give meaning to it (by emotions, memories, etc.), perception occurs.

Sensation and perception work together for a person to be able to identify and create meaning from stimuli-related information. The two elements complement and balance one another. Perception is not possible without sensation; without perception, sensations are left unknown and not understood as there would be no mental processing of what one senses.

One element of growth that is vital to a child's development is that of sensory experiences. Young children learn to integrate the sensations from muscles and joints as well as sensations received through different parts of the body (e.g., hands, knees, mouth, and ears). The sensation of gravity is integrated into a child's learning, and different movements help organize the brain. All of these sensory integrations will be used for play, learning, speech, and motor skill mastery.

The different senses are gustatory (taste), tactile (touch), auditory (hearing), visual (sight), olfactory (smell), proprioception (feedback from the joints and muscles), and vestibular (equilibrium or balance). These last two are what's known as movement-based senses.

Another level of development has to do with a child's ability to receive, interpret, and respond successfully to sensory information. This is known as perceptual motor development. With the sensory motor skills as a foundation for learning and control of the body, the child gathers more sensory information while moving through his/her environment and practices skills to develop coordination and small motor development. Through increasingly complex experiences, the child develops more complex hand-eye coordination, visual-spatial perception, and auditory language skills, which are the foundation for skills needed for daily living as he/she grows into adulthood.

Piaget's Moral Development in Children

(For a more complete discussion of Piaget's theory of cognitive development, please see the section on Piaget in "Methods, Approaches, Ethics, and Assessment.")

Jean Piaget was primarily interested in children's moral reasoning (i.e., what they think about questions of morality) more than what they actually do. The three main areas of children's moral reasoning that interested Piaget were their understanding of rules, moral responsibility, and justice. He noted that children's ideas about all of these aspects of morality evolved as they grew older and that the children passed through stages of moral development, similar to stages of cognitive development. The two types of moral reasoning that Piaget described are heteronomous morality, or moral realism, and autonomous morality, or moral relativism.

Heteronomous morality is morality that is imposed from the outside, such as by parents, teachers, or God. Children in this stage of moral development believe that breaking the rules will lead to immediate and severe punishment and punishment is given to make the guilty suffer in relation to the severity of their wrongdoing. In heteronomous morality, rules are absolute and unchanging, and intentions or reasons for behavior are not taken into account. A small amount of deliberate damage is not as bad as a large amount of accidental damage.

As children mature, they experience a radical change in their attitude toward moral questions. Children who have entered the stage of autonomous morality recognize that morality depends not on consequences but on intentions and that there is no absolute right or wrong. By the age of 9 or 10, children become able to see things from others' point of view and also understand that rules are created by people and can be changed. Older children start to realize that a well-intentioned act that had bad results will likely garner less punishment than malicious intentions that do less harm. Unlike younger children who view punishment as retribution, older children start to see punishment as restitution and that it is necessary to put things right and not just have the guilty suffer. Older children are also more focused on justice and believe that it is always wrong to punish the innocent for others' misdeeds.

Vygotsky

In contrast with Piaget's stages of cognitive and moral development, Vygotsky developed a socio-cultural approach to cognitive development. He asserted that social learning precedes and even leads to development and that community plays a central role in the process of creating meaning. Unlike Piaget, Vygotsky assumes that cognitive development varies across cultures, and he emphasizes the effect of culture on cognitive development. Vygotsky emphasized social factors in development and asserted that children's environment influences how they think and what they think about. He also emphasizes the role of language in cognitive development, which he sees as resulting from an internalization of language.

Havighurst

Robert Havighurst established the theory of human development known as the developmental task concept. This theory asserts that the individual needs to achieve certain tasks at different points in life to continue to develop into a happy and successful adult. Havighurst divides these tasks into three categories: those influenced most by the individual's biology (physiological maturation and genetic makeup), psychology (personal values and goals), or sociology (culture in which the individual belongs). An example of a task influenced most by biology is that of a child learning to crawl, which becomes necessary as a small child matures physically. How an individual establishes his/her self-concept is an example of a task influenced most by psychology or personal values and goals. An individual who lives in an agricultural community will likely seek an occupation such as that of farmer; this is an example of a task influenced most by sociology, or the culture of the individual.

Havighurst proposed a list of common critical tasks categorized into six developmental stages. A few examples from each stage are listed as follows:

Infancy and early childhood (birth to 5 years)

- Learning to walk
- Learning to control bodily functions
- Learning to talk
- Learning to develop relationships with others

Middle childhood (6–12 years)

- Developing physical skills for playing games
- Learning school-related skills such as reading, writing, and counting
- Developing values and conscience
- Becoming more independent

Adolescence (13–17 years)

- Attaining emotional independence from parents
- Developing skills needed for productive occupation
- Establishing mature relationships with peers of both sexes

Early adulthood (18–35 years)

- Choosing a partner
- Establishing a family
- Managing a home
- Establishing a career

Middle age (36–60 years)

- Maintaining economic standard of living
- Performing social and civic responsibilities
- Relating to a spouse or partner as a person
- Adjusting to physiological changes

Later maturity (over 60 years)

- Adjusting to deteriorating health and physical strength
- Adjusting to retirement
- Meeting social and civil obligations
- Adjusting to death or loss of spouse

John Bowlby and Attachment Theory

John Bowlby defined attachment as the "lasting psychological connectedness between human beings." He theorized that infants possess an innate need to form an attachment bond with a caregiver, most likely a parent. Bowlby's work with emotionally disturbed children led him to assert a link between early infant separations from the primary caregiver and later maladjustment. Bowlby observed that children experienced severe distress when separated from their mothers, and even when they were fed by other caregivers their anxiety did not diminish. This appeared to contradict the behavioral theory of attachment, which had been dominant. Bowlby showed that the behavioral theory underestimated the bond that a child has with his/her primary caregiver and that children become attached to their caregivers not only because they are fed by them but

- 73 -

because of the "lasting psychological connectedness" that they have with their caregivers. Bowlby asserted that feeding itself is not the basis or purpose of the attachment bond. A child can develop a sense of trust in the world when attachment figures are available and reliable. Once this happens, the child is able to rely on the caregiver as a secure base from which he/she can explore the world.

Bowlby established that the attachment bond forms in a series of stages—preattachment, attachment-in-the-making, clear-cut attachment, and formation of reciprocal relationships. During the pre-attachment phase, babies can recognize the primary caregiver but do not yet have an attachment formed. Through the caregiver's meeting the infant's needs, by about the age of 3 months, the child will begin to recognize the caregiver more and will develop a sense of trust. During attachment-in-the-making, the infant will show a preference for the primary caregiver as well as for certain secondary caregivers. In clear-cut attachment, a child forms a strong attachment to one individual and will experience separation distress and anxiety when separated from that person. Finally, in the formation of reciprocal relationships, the child will begin to develop strong attachments to people beyond the primary caregivers.

Bowlby's colleague, Mary Ainsworth, identified three types of attachment that a child can demonstrate: secure, avoidant, and resistant/ambivalent. Later Mary Main identified a fourth type—disorganized attachment.

Attachment Theory and the Strange Situation

Despite John Bowlby's belief that attachment was an all-or-nothing process, research has shown that there are individual differences in attachment quality. As mentioned, Mary Ainsworth determined that there are several distinct types of attachment. She came to this conclusion through her research involving an assessment technique called the Strange Situation Classification. This research was conducted to examine how attachments might vary among children. In this study the researchers investigated the security and style of attachment in 1- to 2-year-olds by observing the behavior of infants in various situations including with mother, with baby and a stranger, with baby alone, with mother and baby alone, and with baby and stranger. The children were observed for different types of behaviors including contact seeking and maintaining, avoidance of proximity and contact, exploratory behaviors, and affect displays such as crying or smiling.

Through this study Mary Ainsworth identified three primary attachment styles: secure, insecure avoidant, and insecure ambivalent/resistant. Ainsworth concluded that these different styles were the result of early interactions with the primary caregiver. Ainsworth's colleague Mary Main identified a fourth attachment style, disorganized attachment, at a later time.

Securely attached children show some stranger anxiety (i.e., avoiding a stranger when alone but are friendly when mother is present), are somewhat distressed when their mother leaves them, and are positive and happy when she returns. They also use their mother or primary caregiver as a secure base from which they explore their environment.

Children with an ambivalent or resistant attachment show more significant stranger anxiety and avoid the stranger with or without their caregiver present. They show intense distress when the caregiver leaves and shows interest in him/her but resists contact with him/her when he/she returns, even pushing him/her away at times. A child with this type of attachment cries more and explores less than children of the other two types.

Children with an avoidant or insecure attachment show no distress at a stranger's presence and play normally when the stranger is there. These children show no signs of distress when their caregiver leaves and little interest when he/she returns. If upset, both mother and stranger are able to comfort the child equally well.

The category of disorganized or disoriented attachment was developed when researchers, including Ainsworth, had difficulty fitting some of the children into one of the three categories, and the fourth classification was later added. In the Strange Situation study, the attachment system is generally expected to activate when the caregiver leaves and then returns. If the child's behavior does not appear to be coordinated in a smooth way through the different phases of the study to achieve some kind of proximity with the caregiver, then it is considered disorganized. Disorganized attachment indicates a disruption or flooding of the attachment system, such as by fear. Many of the so-called disorganized infants, however, continue to approach the caregiver and seek comfort from him/her and can cease their distress without ambivalent or avoidant behavior.

Ainsworth concluded that a child's attachment style is dependent on the behavior that his/her caregiver shows toward him/her. Sensitive caregivers are more responsive to their child's needs and respond correctly to their child's moods and feelings. They are more likely to have securely attached children. This is contrasted with caregivers who are less sensitive towards their child, who respond to the child's needs incorrectly, or who are impatient or ignore the child. These caregivers are more likely to have insecurely attached children. These findings of Ainsworth's provided the first empirical evidence for Bowlby's attachment theory.

Approaches to Language Development

The learning theory (behaviorism) approach to language acquisition proposes that language is learned through reinforcement and conditioning. An early explanation for the acquisition of language was given by behaviorist and psychologist B. F. Skinner. Skinner explained the phenomenon of language development as a result of environmental influence. He argued that children learn language due to behaviorist reinforcement by associating words with meaning. He attributed learning to positive reinforcement given to correct utterances, such as asking for milk and receiving it. Children will find the outcome of receiving what they have asked for rewarding, which will enhance their language development. Behaviorism does not fully explain language development as children are able to come up with unique sentence structures on their own and not just those that have been specifically reinforced. It is possible that reinforcement, imitation, and modeling are supplementary to language acquisition instead of the rule.

The nativist approach to language development addresses some of the issues with the learning theory approach to language development. It suggests that learning language is an inborn process and that humans have an innate ability to learn and understand language as well as its more complex structures. Neural cognitive research supports the nativist approach as it has found brain structures related to and responsible for language as well as a gene related to language. Noam Chomsky, the world's most famous linguist to date, heavily criticized Skinner's language development theory. Chomsky argued that language input alone was insufficient to explain how children acquire the tools needed for processing an infinite number of sentences. Chomsky instead proposed his theory of Universal Grammar, which is a scheme of innate biological grammatical categories (such as a noun category and a verb category) that make possible language development in children and language processing in adults. Chomsky theorized that each individual has an innate Language Acquisition Device, which encodes Universal Grammar into a child's brain. Chomsky proposed that the task of the child is to learn the words of his/her particular language; children will instinctively know how to combine nouns and verbs into a meaningful correct phrase due to their inborn Language Acquisition Device.

Finally, the interactionist approach combines different language development theories and suggests that different factors, including both genetics and socialization, are involved in language acquisition. This perspective suggests that there are innate mechanisms in the brain responsible for language development but that they must be activated by environmental and social factors.

The Critical Period Hypothesis proposes that language can develop readily during the first few years of life, and after this time has passed language acquisition is much more difficult or even impossible. There appear to be two distinct cutoffs for the critical period, one around age 5 and the other around the onset of puberty. Those individuals who had little or no language input in their early years (including sign language for deaf individuals) were still able to achieve some fluency if they began exposure to language by the age of 12 (although often not full proficiency). Additionally, early language exposure increases the ability to learn a second language later in life.

Stages of Language Acquisition

Pre-linguistic stage. The first year of life is a pre-speech stage, but the child is developing aspects of communication related to speech, such as gestures, eye contact, sound repartee with the caregiver, cooing, babbling, and crying.

Holophrastic or one-word sentence. A child typically reaches this stage between 10 and 13 months of age. The single-word utterance is also supplemented by the context as well as nonverbal cues, such as pointing.

Two-word sentence. Children typically reach this stage by 18 months, and their utterances usually contain a noun or verb plus a modifier. Sentences can be declarative (car fast), interrogative (where Mommy?), negative (no bread), or imperative (more cake!). Like in the holophrastic stage, context and nonverbal communication support the meaning of the utterance.

Multiple-word sentence. Between the age of 2 and 2 1/2, the child will reach this stage. Use of grammatical morphemes like prefixes or suffixes can be used when changing meanings or tenses. Additionally, the child can now form sentences with a subject and a predicate. The examples from the previous stage might be expanded thusly: car is fast, where is Mommy?, that is not bread, I want more cake. Examples of utilizing a prefix or a suffix are: I catched it, I falling.

More complex grammatical structures. A child will reach this stage between approximately 2 1/2 and 3 years old. At this time, they will start to use more complex and intricate grammatical structures; additional elements such as conjunctions are added, embedded, and permuted within sentences, and prepositions are used. Some examples include conjunction (throw it, my ball), embedding (where is Brother?), permutation (I can't play), and preposition (Take me to the park).

Adult-like language structures. This level is reached by the typical 5- to 6-year-old child. Utterances now include more complex structural distinctions, such as with ask, tell, or promise, and word orders are changed appropriately (ask him where they went, she promised to help me).

Emotional Development

Emotional development in children is strongly connected to cognitive development. Although people often see the two as distinct parts of learning and becoming, in reality they are intertwined. Childhood emotional development depends quite strongly on the quality of relationships that a child has with his/her caregivers and teachers and on the interactions with those adults. Healthy emotional development affects the ability of a person to function successfully as an adult not only in social spheres but also academically and professionally.

Aspects of emotional development include understanding a person's own feelings, perceiving and understanding the feelings of others, dealing with one's feelings in a healthy way, being able to manage one's behavior, learning to have empathy for other people, and developing and sustaining healthy relationships with others. As children grow from infancy to adulthood, both the complexity of their emotions increases as well as their ability to deal with more and more ambiguity in their own and others' emotions.

In the first 3 months of a child's life, emotional development centers around learning about one's own self as well as about the other people in one's surroundings. At this stage, an infant is starting to learn that he/she is an individual and separate from those around him/her. Infants at this age also learn about their own bodies (looking at their hands, sucking on their fingers, and paying attention to parts of their body that a caregiver is touching), how different kinds of touch feel, how different parts of their body are attached (i.e., arms and legs), how caregivers can soothe and comfort them, and how to enjoy social stimulation.

As infants grow, they have a base of understanding about their own bodies, and social interaction becomes more and more important. Infants from 3 to 6 months of age smile, laugh, and even learn their own name and respond when they hear it. The game of peekaboo comes into play at this stage. As they grow, they begin to prefer familiar people over those they don't know as well. Children from ages 6 to 9 months of age know the difference between members of their family and strangers. They also respond when people speak or gesture to them. Their emotions start to become more complex, and they can express anger, happiness, fear, and sadness, among others. Children who are between 9 and 12 months of age not only show a preference for their caregivers, but they actually show distress when separated from them. At this age they are learning more self-regulation along with more complex physical skills such as feeding themselves and imitating others.

Children between 1 and 2 years of age increase the amount of self-awareness that they have. They can recognize themselves in a mirror. They also take part in many new play activities, including initiating play, playing independently, and imitating caregivers' actions in their play. They can express pleasure when they accomplish things, express frustration or anger, and even try to give others directions.

Between ages 2 and 4 years old, children greatly increase their self-confidence and independence. Just as they are able to successfully complete more and more complicated physical tasks, they are also able to interact socially and emotionally in increasingly complex ways. Children at this age express their preferences for many things, including food and toys. They say "no," are possessive of their belongings, and increasingly learn to share with others. They can have rapid mood changes. They learn to follow directions, play with other children, and take part in pretend games.

As children move out of the preschool years, they have increasing awareness of others. They make friends with other children and become much more responsive to the feelings of others. They learn about good and bad actions and learn to compare themselves to others. Early childhood brings an understanding of what embarrassment is and more attention paid to the responses of others. As children grow older into middle childhood and pre-adolescence, they increasingly seek to establish their own identity. They can still be childlike and silly at times but can also be selfish and argumentative as they start learning to increase their independence. Pre-adolescents have a greater ability to process cognitive complexities, and this is mirrored in their ability to navigate more and more complex social situations as well. They can differentiate among different expressions of themselves with different social groups (i.e., family, close friends, and acquaintances).

As kids move into adolescence, they are able to think more logically, although they may be quite moody and often need privacy. The opinions of peers become even more important to them, and the opinions of caregivers and family members take on less importance. Adolescents may "try on" different personality traits or style choices in attempts to figure themselves out. In seeking independence from parental figures, adolescents typically become emotionally distant. This is all a part of individuation and learning to become a healthy and competent adult, although the process may be painful for both adolescent and parent.

Kohlberg's Theory of Moral Development

Twenty-five years after Piaget presented his theory of moral development, Lawrence Kohlberg put forward his own theory of moral development. At the time, behaviorism and psychoanalysis were the primary psychological approaches; these both attributed morality to the internalization of family and societal rules through reinforcement or identification with authority. In contrast, Kohlberg emphasized the importance of an individual's own reasoning in making moral judgments.

To study moral development, Kohlberg would introduce moral dilemmas to people in his studies. Based on their responses, he would place them in one of six stages, which are split into three levels. The three levels are pre-conventional morality, conventional morality, and post-conventional morality. As a person advances through the stages, Kohlberg would assert that they are increasingly better at dealing with moral dilemmas than they were in previous stages.

Pre-conventional moral reasoning is mostly seen in children, although not exclusively. This level is less about right and wrong than about the consequences brought about by the actions in question. The stages in this level are (1) obedience and punishment orientation and (2) self-interest orientation. In Stage 1 the individual seeks to avoid immoral behavior because he/she may be punished. The severity of the punishment determines how bad or immoral an action may be. In Stage 2 the individual begins to pay attention to others' needs but only as far as the individual's own interests are advanced. This level does not take into account the greater community interest but rather only the interests of the individual.

Conventional moral reasoning is the usual level for adults and adolescents. As a person comes into this second level, he/she comes to accept what the greater society declares to be right or wrong. He/she may follow rules somewhat strictly without examining whether the rules are just or right. The stages in this level are (3) good interpersonal relationships and (4) maintaining the social order. In Stage 3 the individual wants others to see him/her as good, and he/she begins to determine how moral an action is based on its effects on relationships with others. The person in Stage 3 does not want others to disapprove of him/her, and so he/she tries to follow the rules. In Stage 4 the individual does not depend on the individual approval of others, as in Stage 3. The person in Stage 4 sees the greater importance of following societal rules and norms for the good of society as a whole.

Post-conventional moral reasoning takes the focus off of society's rules and norms and shifts it to the individual's own moral perspective. In this level, the individual may end up disobeying rules when they conflict with his/her own ethical principles. For people in this level, rules can be questioned and even disobeyed when they are deemed to be unjust. The stages in this level are (5) social contract and individual rights and (6) universal ethical principles. The person in Stage 5 sees rules and laws as social contracts and not as unbending mandates. He/she would change rules that are unjust or that serve to harm individuals or groups. The person in Stage 6 sees rules or laws that are unjust as invalid. He/she believes that he/she is obligated break or defy unjust rules, even if he/she must face societal or legal consequences for doing so.

The most famous moral dilemma that Kohlberg used in his research is that of Heinz, a man with an ill wife. The drug that she needs has been priced far above what Heinz can afford and many times more than what it cost to produce. After unsuccessfully pleading with the pharmacist to sell him the drug at an affordable price or allow him to pay later, Heinz decides to break into the laboratory to steal the drug so that his wife can have it and be cured. The question for research participants was whether or not Heinz should have broken in to steal this drug. How participants answer this dilemma and their stated reasoning for their answer determines their stage of moral reasoning.

Gilligan's Theory of Moral Development

Carol Gilligan has pioneered the field of gender difference psychology, which argues that men and women tend to think differently, in particular about moral problems. She asserts that these differences are likely due to gender conditioning and social influences. She argues that women's ways of thinking are often undervalued by society compared to those of men.

Gilligan is best known for her adaptation of Kohlberg's theory of moral development. Kohlberg found that more men reached the highest levels of moral reasoning. He also found that men strongly focused on justice. Gilligan criticized Kohlberg's theory as biased in favor of men. In her research, Gilligan found that women place a stronger emphasis on the role of caring in moral decision-making, something that Kohlberg's theory does not allow for. Because of this, women often fail to reach Kohlberg's so-called higher stages of moral reasoning.

Gilligan asserts that a woman's morality is influenced by her relationships and that women take into account how their decisions will affect others when forming their moral and ethical foundation. Like Kohlberg, Gilligan believes that women develop morality in stages, and she utilizes Kohlberg's phrasing of pre-conventional, conventional, and post-conventional. She has, however, based her stages on her research with women, and they vary from Kohlberg's stages significantly. In Gilligan's pre-conventional morality stage, the goal is individual survival. The individual then transitions from a focus on selfishness to a feeling of responsibility for others. In the conventional stage, self-sacrifice is seen as goodness. The individual then transitions from this focus on goodness to the truth that she (the individual herself) is a person, too, and worthy of caring. In the post-conventional stage, women emphasize taking responsibility for the consequences of their choices and gaining control of their own lives. Caring for others remains a strong component of this highest stage of moral development.

Factors That Interact With the Process of Development

There are many factors that affect the social and emotional development rate of children. These factors include the following.

- *Environmental risk factors:* unsafe living conditions or community, low-quality child care, lack of community resources, lack of policies supporting children and families, and so on. Maternal use of alcohol or drugs while pregnant can have a strong impact on a child's development by causing fetal alcohol syndrome or other issues.
- *Family risk factors:* maternal depression, mental illness or substance abuse in the family, family violence, poverty, and so on. Many of these stressful factors can actually affect the growth in parts of the brain involved in stress regulation, emotional processing, and memory.

- *Within-child risk factors:* fussy temperament, developmental delay, and serious health issues. Developmental delays can have genetic causes (such as Down syndrome), complications of pregnancy and birth (such as prematurity or infections), or unknown causes. Some causes of developmental delay are reversible if caught early enough, such as hearing loss from chronic ear infections.

Intelligence Theories and Testing

Although there is no standard definition of what intelligence is, many researchers have come up with different explanations. Some assert that intelligence is a single, general ability; others believe that it includes an array of aptitudes, talents, and skills. Definitions of intelligence vary greatly, but a general understanding of intelligence is that it involves the ability to learn, recognize problems, and solve problems. Different mental abilities that intelligence encompasses include logic, reasoning, problem-solving, and planning. Intelligence is a topic that is highly researched but also generates great controversy, for example, the use of testing to screen job applicants or to identify children who need academic help.

The first intelligence tests were developed by Alfred Binet to assist the French government in identifying schoolchildren who needed extra help with schoolwork. German psychologist William Stern first coined the phrase *intelligence quotient*, or IQ, in the early 1900s.

Over the past hundred years, researchers have formulated the following theories of intelligence.

General Intelligence

Charles Spearman, a British psychologist, believed that there was an underlying intelligence factor that influenced outcomes in types of cognitive tasks. He called this general intelligence or the *g* factor. Spearman found that people who do well in certain cognitive areas (such as math) also tend to do well in other areas (such as reading) and likewise for those who perform poorly. He asserted that this "general intelligence" can be measured and described numerically. In pursuit of understanding the *g* factor, Spearman helped develop the statistical theory called factor analysis.

Other Theories of Intelligence—Sternberg, Thurstone, and Gardner

Some theorists have posited that intelligence is not a singular factor but as a more nuanced and varied set of abilities. Instead of one particular quality determining how intelligent a person is in various domains, these different domains each represent their own type of intelligence.

Robert J. Sternberg's triarchic theory of intelligence describes mental functions as a set of metacomponents or triarchic components. These three factors or components include the following:

- Problem-solving ability or analytical intelligence
- Experiential or creative intelligence, which deals with the ability to react to new situations and challenges
- Practical intelligence, which deals with creating the best fit between oneself and the environment, also known as "street smarts"

In a similar vein, Louis L. Thurstone proposed the theory of primary mental abilities. This set of abilities stands in contrast to the *g* factor. In any single individual, different abilities may be stronger or weaker, leading to a more diverse view of intelligence. Thurstone's primary mental abilities include the following:

- Verbal comprehension
- Word fluency
- Numerical ability
- Spatial relations, memory
- Perceptual speed
- Reasoning

Howard Gardner posited a theory of multiple intelligences that he believed more fully represents the varied abilities of people. Different cultures value distinct skills and abilities to varying degrees. Gardner's eight intelligence modalities include the following:

- Visual-spatial
- Musical-rhythmic and harmonic
- Verbal-linguistic
- Bodily-kinesthetic
- Interpersonal
- Intrapersonal
- Logical-mathematical
- Naturalistic

Questions Remain

Much about intelligence and IQ testing is theoretical and unproven. Some important questions about this area of study include the following:

- How much of intelligence is a single ability, and how much encompasses a multitude of abilities and skills?
- What roles do genetics and environment play in intelligence?
- What biases may intelligence tests have?
- Can intelligence scores predict something about people, and if so, what?

Stanford-Binet Intelligence Scales

This series of tests helps assess cognitive strengths and weaknesses and is a tool used to evaluate if a student has a learning disability. The Stanford-Binet can be used with people from ages 2 to 85. It measures five different factors of cognitive ability:

- Fluid reasoning
- Knowledge
- Quantitative reasoning
- Visual-spatial processing
- Working memory

The Stanford-Binet is used to diagnose a wide range of developmental disabilities and is also useful in the following contexts:

- Clinical and neuropsychological assessment
- Early childhood assessment

- Psycho-educational evaluations for special education placement
- Providing information for interventions like Individual Education Programs, career assessment, adult neuropsychological treatment, and others
- Adult social security and workers' compensation evaluations
- Forensic contexts
- Research on abilities and aptitudes

Wechsler Adult Intelligence Scale (WAIS)

The Wechsler Adult Intelligence Scale (WAIS) is established on David Wechsler's idea of intelligence, which he describes as "the global capacity of a person to act purposefully, to think rationally, and to deal effectively with his environment." Wechsler asserted that intelligence was comprised of specific elements that can be isolated, defined, and measured. He did not see these elements as independent but rather as interrelated. He argues that general intelligence is made up of specific and interrelated functions that can be individually measured.

These ideas about intelligence varied significantly from the Binet scale, commonly seen as the highest authority in intelligence testing at the time. Wechsler strongly advocated for the concept of non-intellective factors, and he asserted that the 1937 version of the Binet scale was lacking in its failure to incorporate these factors into the scale. Non-intellective factors include things like lack of confidence, fear of failure, attitudes, and so on and contribute to the overall score in intelligence but are not in and of themselves intelligence-related items. Other criticisms Wechsler had of the Binet scale include the single score that it gave, its design being for children not adults, and the emphasis on speed.

A critical difference from the Binet scale was the nonverbal performance scale. The Binet scale had been relentlessly criticized for emphasizing language and verbal scales. Because of this, Wechsler created an entire scale that allowed the measurement of nonverbal intelligence, which became known as the performance scale. In essence, this scale required the subject to perform a task (like copy symbols or point out a missing detail) rather than simply answer questions. This development in assessment was important as it attempted to overcome biases caused by language, education, and culture. Additionally, the performance scale allowed clinicians to observe subjects completing a type of behavior that required something physical as well as a longer interval of sustained effort and attention.

The Wechsler-Bellevue scale was first released in 1939 and has been revised several times. The current version is the WAIS IV. Many of the original concepts that Wechsler advocated for have now become standards in psychological testing.

Wechsler Intelligence Scale for Children (WISC)

Although the Wechsler Intelligence Scale for Children (WAIS) is used for persons 16 and older, the WISC is aimed at persons between 6 and 16 years of age. It can be used to determine if a child is achieving below what one would expect, which may be explained by learning disabilities. Evaluators also use the WISC to compare a child's age with his/her cognitive development and can help identify intellectual weaknesses and strengths, including "giftedness." From the results of the WISC, both a "full-scale IQ" as well as five primary index scores are given. The five indices are: verbal comprehension, visual spatial, fluid reasoning, working memory, and processing speed.

Cultural Bias in Testing

Categories of testing bias include construct-validity bias, content-validity bias, and predictive-validity bias.

Whether a test accurately measures what it was designed to is known as construct-validity bias. For example, students who are English language learners may encounter words they haven't yet learned on intelligence tests, and therefore the test results may be reflective of their English language skills rather than intellectual abilities.

When the content of a test is comparatively more difficult for one group of students than for others it is known as content-validity bias. This occurs in the following scenarios: when members of a subgroup of test takers (e.g., ethnic minority groups) have not had the same opportunity to learn the material that is being tested, when scoring is unfair to a group (e.g., when answers that make sense in one group's culture are scored as incorrect), or when the wording of questions is unfamiliar to test takers because of cultural or linguistic differences. A subcategory of content-validity bias is item-selection bias. This refers to the use of individual testing items that are more appropriate for one group's language and cultural experiences than to others.

A test's accuracy in predicting how well a group of test takers will perform in the future is known as predictive-validity bias or bias in criterion-related validity. An example of this would be a test's being considered unbiased if it was able to predict future academic and test performance equally well for all groups of students.

Some believe that certain tests are culturally loaded and that their language and content give an unfair advantage to test takers of the dominant culture. Some believe that many tests do not actually measure aptitude but rather the knowledge of mainstream white culture. Those who support this view acknowledge that minority children and children from the dominant culture are raised in different environments and learn different values and skills that are needed to succeed in their respective cultures. Some assert that a universal, unbiased test is not possible to achieve. Those on the other side of this argument assert that testing is valid and accurately measures intelligence and predicts future achievement.

Psychological Disorders

Problems with mental health often have a variety of causes: genetic factors, environmental stresses, biochemical imbalances, or a combination. Mental illness is often physical as well as psychological and emotional. Researchers do not know the exact cause of most mental illnesses; however, it is becoming increasingly clear through increased study that a combination of many factors contributes to them. Although in the past it was believed that mental health problems were caused by personal weakness or defects of character, scientists now know that at their root are genetic, biological, environmental, and psychological causes.

Many mental illnesses seem to run in families. This suggests that they may be passed on from generation to generation genetically. This does not mean that a child of a person with mental illness will necessarily have one as well. Heredity in this case means that a person is more likely to have the condition than if he/she did not have an affected family member. Additionally, researchers have come to believe that many mental health conditions are linked to issues in multiple genes, not merely one. This helps explain why a person can inherit a susceptibility to a mental disorder, but the disorder doesn't always manifest itself. A combination of genes and other factors, including environmental stressors and psychological trauma, can trigger a mental illness in a person who has inherited susceptibility to it.

- 83 -

A link has been found between some mental illnesses and an abnormal balance of neurotransmitters, which are chemicals in the brain. Neurotransmitters assist in communication among brain cells, and if they are out of balance or aren't working as they should, this communication may break down. This can lead to symptoms of mental illness. In some cases, defects in or injury to the brain have been linked to some mental illnesses.

Common Symptoms of Mental Disorders

Generally speaking, one or two symptoms are not enough for a mental health diagnosis. Rather, those with mental illness typically present a collection of symptoms. These symptoms must be persistent and interfere with daily life and work. What follows is an educational and informational tool and is not a diagnostic instrument. Some general symptoms are associated with mental health problems and psychological disorders.

In adults we might see the following:

- Social withdrawal
- Prolonged depression (which can manifest as sadness or irritability)
- Excessive worries, anxieties, or fears
- Obvious changes in sleeping or eating habits
- Feelings of extremes—both highs and lows
- Confused thinking
- Strong anger
- Suicidal thoughts
- Delusions or hallucinations
- Substance abuse
- Increasing inability to cope with problems and activities of daily life
- Denial of obvious problems
- Unexplained physical ailments

In children or pre-adolescents, we might see the following:

- Changes in school performance
- Poor grades in spite of great effort
- Changes in sleeping and/or eating habits
- Persistent worry or anxiety
- Persistent disobedience, aggression, or defiance of authority
- Frequent temper tantrums
- Excessive complains of physical ailments
- Frequent outbursts of anger
- Inability to cope with daily activities and problems
- Persistent negative mood, sometimes accompanied by thoughts of death
- Hyperactivity
- Persistent nightmares

Major Categories of Mental Illnesses

There are many different types of mental illness as the definition is so broad. The most recent edition of the *Diagnostic and Statistical Manual of Mental Disorders* (DSM-5) divides mental illness into five different types. These five different types are collections of disorders based on developmental and life span factors as well as the nature of the disorders themselves. The five broad categories of the disorders described in the DSM-5 are as follows:

1. *Neurodevelopmental disorders*—these are brain and nervous system disorders that have their onset during the early stages of development.
2. *Internalizing disorders*—these primarily manifest internally; symptoms are turned inward within the person. These include anxiety disorders, depressive disorders, and sometimes eating disorders (which can also be externalizing).
3. *Externalizing disorders*—these manifest externally with the behaviors turned outward toward the world. These include conduct disorder, substance abuse, and the manic phase of bipolar disorder.
4. *Neurocognitive disorders*—disorders and diseases of the brain can contribute to a decline in cognitive processing and functioning.
5. *Other disorders*—these are other conditions that do not meet the required diagnostic criteria for a specific mental illness such as a mood or anxiety disorder; however, these do cause significant dysfunction and disruption.

These five categories are simply a framing device to help organize the many disorders that are covered in the DSM. What follows is further discussion of many of these disorders.

Neurodevelopmental Disorders

Neurodevelopmental disorders are usually diagnosed early in life—during infancy, childhood, or adolescence. They involve problems during development, particularly with the brain. Some examples of neurodevelopmental disorders include the following:

- *Attention deficit hyperactivity disorder (ADHD)*—constant and long-standing behavior pattern evidenced by problems with inattention, a tendency toward impulsiveness, and hyperactivity. These symptoms make it difficult for a person to perform appropriately in two or more areas of life, beginning before age 12.
- *Autism spectrum disorder*—consists of a wide array of symptoms affecting social interactions, communication, and behavioral patterns. It begins in early childhood and can cause repetitive or restrictive behavior, including compulsive behavior, repetitive movements, and resistance to change. Because it is a spectrum disorder, severity varies widely, and individuals may have different levels of functioning.
- *Intellectual development disorder*—individuals have low IQ levels (at or below 70, possibly as high as 75), problems with cognitive functioning, and limitations in basic life skills (i.e., self-care, social skills, etc.). The disorder begins before age 18 and sometimes goes along with other medical symptoms (syndromic, such as Down's syndrome) or without any other issues (non-syndromic). Previously this was referred to as mental retardation. Before the age of 5, children may be temporarily diagnosed with global developmental delay, until which time their IQ can be tested.
- *Other neurodevelopmental disorders*—these include learning disorders (also called learning disabilities), communication disorders (such as stuttering or language disorders), motor disorders, and traumatic brain injury.

Schizophrenia Spectrum and Other Psychotic Disorders

The primary symptom in this category is psychosis, or an episodic break from reality, primarily hallucinations (sensing things that are not there) and delusions (believing things that aren't true). Other symptoms include incoherent speech, abnormal reasoning, and social withdrawal. Examples

- 85 -

of these disorders include delusional disorder, brief psychotic disorder, schizophrenia, and schizoaffective disorder.

Depressive Disorders

These disorders are characterized by prolonged depressed mood, loss of interest in activities, changes in appetite or weight, changes in sleeping habits, feelings of worthlessness, impaired memory or concentration, fatigue, and thoughts of suicide. Disorders in this category include major depressive disorder (both single episode and recurrent), persistent depressive disorder (dysthymia), and premenstrual depressive disorder.

Bipolar Disorder

In the past, bipolar disorder was called manic depression as those who have it experience shifts between depression and mania, which is marked by an elevated, even hyper mood and increased energy levels among other symptoms. People experiencing mania often act in risky ways that may have lasting consequences, such as gambling, sexual promiscuity, and uncontrolled spending, among others. Bipolar II disorder presents with a less severe form of mania called hypomania, along with depression. Those with bipolar can have episodes (of either depression or mania/hypomania) that last for months; they can cycle rapidly, experiencing multiple cycles during one day or anywhere in between.

Anxiety Disorders

The disorders in this category cause distressing and frequent periods of fear and apprehension lasting 6 months or more. Symptoms include panic attacks, physical symptoms (nausea, pain, and headaches), obsessive thoughts, difficulty sleeping, nightmares, and fear of leaving the house. Examples of anxiety disorders include the following:

- *Generalized anxiety disorder*—a quite common disorder, particularly in older adults, it is marked by persistent and nonspecific anxiety and also excessive worry about everyday things. It can cause impairment in making regular decisions, difficulties with memory due to poor concentration, and also physical symptoms such as fatigue and sleep problems.
- *Panic disorder*—panic attacks are brief episodes of extreme fear and anxiety that often include physical symptoms such as difficulty breathing, dizziness, nausea, and so on. People with panic disorder experience panic attacks, often with no known trigger, and may live in dread of the next attack. People with panic disorder may spend much time and energy attempting to stave off attacks or avoid possible triggers. The panic attacks themselves become a source of anxiety.
- *Social anxiety disorder*—this disorder involves fear of social situations in which one may be watched, judged, and/or embarrassed. It can cause difficulties with making friends and can lead to social isolation when the person seeks to avoid the triggering situation (i.e., social situations).
- *Separation anxiety disorder*—although separation anxiety is normal in infants and children, an excessive or inappropriate anxiety upon separation from a caregiver or other person or place qualifies as a disorder. Both children and adults have this disorder, but it tends to be more severe in children.
- *Agoraphobia*—closely connected to panic disorder, people with agoraphobia have a fear of public spaces, or a place where they are unable to escape or get help. Panic attacks can trigger agoraphobia as the individual seeks to avoid activities or places where he/she may have an attack.

- *Specific phobias*—this is the largest category of anxiety disorders and involves fear of specific situations or things. People experience fear far out of proportion to the actual risk. Different types of phobias include those of natural events (such as storms), medical issues (such as certain procedures or instruments), animals (such as spiders or dogs), and situational (such as flying or enclosed spaces).

Obsessive-Compulsive and Related Disorders

Disorders in this category are characterized by extreme recurrent thoughts or preoccupations that are connected to either mental or behavioral behaviors, which are done to alleviate the obsessions. In addition to obsessive-compulsive disorder, examples include hoarding disorder, body dysmorphic disorder, trichotillomania (hair-pulling disorder), and excoriation (skin picking disorder), among others.

Trauma- and Stressor-Related Disorders

Disorders in this category were previously grouped with anxiety disorders but are now in a distinct category of their own. They involve exposure to a stressful or traumatic event and are mental disorders resulting from outside forces that impact or alter the brain itself. Examples include the following:

- *Reactive attachment disorder*—now subdivided into two distinct disorders, reactive attachment disorder and disinhibited social engagement disorder, both are caused when a child does not form a healthy attachment to his/her primary caregiver in the first few years of life. Symptoms of reactive attachment disorder include withdrawal and lack of social engagement, social and emotional disturbances, listlessness, and sadness. Disinhibited social engagement disorder causes a child to not have discomfort with strangers and not see the caregiver as a safe and secure person, which can lead to dangerous situations.
- *Adjustment disorder*—this is an abnormal response to a life stressor or sudden change, such as death of a loved one, divorce, job loss, or another setback. Despite struggling to adjust, the person experiences impacts in multiple areas of life, such as relationships and work.
- *Posttraumatic stress disorder (PTSD)*—following a disturbing and stressful life event (either experienced or witnessed), some people develop symptoms such as re-experiencing the event (i.e., flashbacks), negative thoughts and mood (i.e., depression), heightened arousal (i.e., hypervigilance and sleep disturbances), and avoidance. PTSD can greatly interfere with one's life, even leading to social isolation, substance abuse, and increased risk for suicide.
- *Acute stress disorder*—similar to PTSD, this disorder occurs 3 days to 1 month after the precipitating event. Some people with acute stress disorder go on to develop PTSD but not all.

Dissociative Disorders

Dissociation is a coping mechanism albeit a pathologic and involuntary one. After a stressful or traumatic situation (either repeated or a one-time incident), a person may experience a break in normal awareness and may have a changed sense of memory, consciousness, or even identity. These disorders are much more common than once thought, and they are frequently diagnosed as other disorders. Every area of cognitive functioning can be affected by dissociation. Types of dissociative disorders include the following:

- *Dissociative identity disorder*—formerly called multiple personality disorder and caused by repeated and continuing trauma occurring before age 9
- *Dissociative amnesia*—caused by a trauma or stressful event and now includes dissociative fugue
- *Depersonalization disorder*—characterized by feeling detached from one's own self or one's surroundings

Somatic Symptom and Related Disorders

Formerly called somatoform or somatization disorders, these involve physical symptoms for which there is no obvious physical or medical cause as well as distress in response to the symptoms. The diagnosis requires that the person have experienced the symptoms over at least 6 months (although not necessarily for the entire time). Forms of somatic symptom disorder include the following:

- *Somatic symptom disorder*—an individual has one or more symptoms that are disrupting normal functioning and cause great distress. Onset is usually before or by age 30.
- *Illness anxiety disorder*—involving a disproportionate worry about having an undiagnosed medical condition, individuals are often excessively preoccupied about how they feel and about their bodily functions. It was previously called hypochondriasis.
- *Conversion disorder*—this disorder involves actual neurologic symptoms such as blindness, paralysis, or numbness.
- *Factitious disorder*—this occurs when a person consciously creates symptoms for a physical or mental illness, such as by self-injury. Individuals do not create symptoms for any practical benefit, such as a lawsuit; instead the benefit is psychological—they need to be seen as sick or hurt. It was previously called Munchausen syndrome.
- *Factitious disorder imposed on another*—previously called Munchausen by proxy, this disorder involves claiming or causing injury or illness in another person, often a child or another dependent.

Feeding and Eating Disorders

Feeding and eating disorders describes conditions in which there is an extreme preoccupation with weight and food, and this preoccupation causes physical and mental health problems. These disorders often co-occur with anxiety disorders or obsessive compulsive disorder. These disorders can cause significant medical problems, including weakened bones, cardiovascular problems, dental problems due to binging, and even loss of brain mass. Proper nutrition is essential to life, and so these disorders can affect every part of a person's health. Types of eating and feeding disorders include the following:

- *Anorexia nervosa*—individuals with this disorder often believe themselves to be of a much higher weight than they actually are. Characterized by an extreme fear of being fat, anorexia nervosa can cause one to greatly restrict food intake, exercise obsessively, and even create bizarre and complex rules for oneself around eating and food.
- *Bulimia nervosa*—individuals with bulimia nervosa will eat large amounts of food and then engage in some activity to compensate for it. Many force themselves to vomit or abuse laxatives and diuretics; others exercise excessively.

- *Binge eating disorder*—this is the newest category of eating disorder but also thought to be the most common. Individuals with this disorder will eat an extremely large amount of food over a short period of time, often in response to an emotional state. Those who have this typically feel they have a lack of control around food and are caused great distress by their binging.
- *Pica*—most typical in children and people with developmental disabilities (although not exclusively), this disorder is characterized by eating nonfood substances such as dirt, paper, soap, chalk, and so on.
- *Rumination disorder*—individuals with this disorder regurgitate food they have just swallowed and re-chew it. They then either spit it out or re-swallow it. Like pica, it mostly occurs in children or adults with developmental disabilities. Because of the repeated regurgitation, individuals can develop serious dental problems and malnutrition, among other issues.

Disruptive, Impulse-Control, and Conduct Disorders

Individuals with disorders in this category are frequently unable to control their emotions or behaviors and experience disruption in multiple areas of their lives. Unlike most of the other disorders discussed here, individuals with these disorders direct their disruptive behavior toward others, often violating others' rights and experiencing great conflict with both peers and authorities. Males are more likely to experience these types of disorders than females. Types of these disorders include the following:

- *Oppositional defiant disorder (ODD)*—this disorder begins in childhood or adolescence, before age 18. It is characterized by a chronic refusal to comply with rules and open defiance of authority figures. Individuals with ODD often blame others for problems they have caused and often seek to deliberately aggravate others.
- *Conduct disorder*—although similar to ODD, this is a more serious disorder and is characterized by more violent and aggressive behavior. Individuals with conduct disorder are more likely to be violent with people or animals and are more likely to destroy property, along with other violations of rules and norms. It can often lead to serious legal problems and great difficulties with forming healthy relationships.
- *Intermittent explosive disorder (IED)*—individuals with IED exhibit sudden bouts of unpremeditated rage and even violence disproportionate to the situation that prompts the explosion. It can begin in childhood, adolescence, or young adulthood and sometimes co-occurs with other disorders, such as bipolar disorder or anxiety disorders.
- *Kleptomania*—individuals with kleptomania have an uncontrollable urge to steal things, often unnecessary items of little value. Despite not wanting to steal, those with this disorder find themselves unable to resist the impulse to steal. Kleptomania can cause significant legal and social problems for these individuals.
- *Pyromania*—individuals with this disorder are preoccupied with setting fires and often endanger themselves and others. As with other impulse-control disorders, individuals with pyromania experience a building tension and then a release after setting a fire.

Substance-Related and Addictive Disorders

Substance-related disorders occur when a person's use of substances increases and begins to affect other areas of their life. These substances may be prescription, over-the-counter substances, legal recreational substances, or illegal recreational substances. These can include alcohol, opioids, hallucinogens, tobacco, and stimulants, among others. The DSM-5 also includes gambling in this addictive disorders category because gambling stimulates the same reward system in the brain that substance misuse does.

Neurocognitive Disorders

Previously referred to as dementia, neurocognitive disorders are characterized by a deterioration of mental abilities that impacts one's daily life. The DSM-5 describes these disorders as either minor or major, depending on their severity. Symptoms include difficulties with cognition, including memory, planning abilities, focusing, and social interactions. Alzheimer's is the largest category of these disorders, but there are multiple other disorders that affect cognitive functioning in a similar way. Some of these disorders also affect the body in other ways, including the ability to control motor skills. Neurocognitive disorders include the following:

- Alzheimer's disease
- Parkinson's disease
- Lewy body disease
- Frontotemporal degeneration
- Huntington's disease
- Prion disease
- Traumatic brain injury (TBI)
- Vascular disease
- Neurocognitive problems caused by HIV

Personality Disorders

The DSM-5 places personality disorders in a separate section than other mental illnesses due to there being a lack of consensus about the nature of these disorders. Personality disorders involve a rigid pattern of behaviors that is in conflict with cultural and social expectations. People with personality disorders exhibit destructive ways of thinking, behaving, and interacting with other people. Personality disorders can co-occur with other disorders, particularly substance abuse disorders and depression.

There are three groupings of personality disorders in the DSM-5. The first group or cluster includes personality disorders that involve eccentric or odd behavior and thinking. Cluster A includes the following:

- Paranoid personality disorder
- Schizoid personality disorder
- Schizotypal personality disorder

Cluster B includes personality disorders that involve erratic, unpredictable, and dramatic thoughts and behavior. Cluster B includes the following:

- Antisocial personality disorder
- Borderline personality disorder
- Histrionic personality disorder
- Narcissistic personality disorder

Cluster C includes personality disorders that involve anxious and fearful thoughts and behavior. Cluster C includes the following:

- Avoidant personality disorder
- Dependent personality disorder
- Obsessive compulsive personality disorder (differs from obsessive compulsive disorder)

Additional Disorders

Other disorders not included in these categories include the following:

- *Sleep-wake disorders*—the sleep-wake cycle is disrupted in some way, affecting how a person is able to function during waking hours.
- *Gender dysphoria*—a person experiences him/herself as a gender other than the one that was assigned to them at birth.
- *Sexual dysfunctions and disorders*—the prevent a person/couple from experiencing sexual pleasure and include arousal disorders, desire disorders, pain disorders, and orgasm disorders.
- *Paraphilic disorders*—these sexual behaviors (including fantasies) involve atypical situations or objects and cause distress or threaten the well-being of another person.
- *Elimination disorders*—these involve the passing of urine (*enuresis*) or feces (*encopresis*), deliberately or not, in an inappropriate way (into clothing, onto the bed or floor, etc.).

Utilizing the DSM-5

The newest version of the *Diagnostic and Statistical Manual of Mental Disorders* (DSM) is the DSM-5, published in 2013. Perhaps the most significant change to this version of the DSM is the discontinuation of the Axis system used in previous editions. Instead, the DSM-5 has 20 chapters of related disorders, arranged more or less in life-span fashion. The DSM-5 consists of three sections. The first provides an introduction to the edition and information about how it is organized. Also, in Section I is information about revisions, field trials, and reviews—public, professional, and expert. In Section II one can find the diagnostic criteria and codes. The coding in the DSM-5 is based on the *International Classification of Diseases, 9th edition, Clinical Modification* (ICD-9-CM) and takes into account the changes made in the ICD-10-CM. The disorders in Section II are summarized in previous sections. The third section deals with measures of assessment, cultural formulations, a glossary, and conditions that call for further study.

Treatment of Psychological Disorders

Psychologist and others who treat psychological disorders typically rely on one or more theoretical frameworks of psychotherapy. These frameworks serve as a type of road map for practitioners and guide them through the process of both understanding their clients and developing solutions. There are five broad categories or theoretical frameworks.

- *Psychoanalysis and psychodynamic therapies.* This framework centers on changing problematic feelings, thoughts, and behaviors through studying their unconscious motivations and meanings. In this approach there is a close working partnership between patient and therapist, and patients learn about themselves through exploring their interactions in this partnership.

- *Behavior therapy.* This method centers on the role of learning in developing behaviors, both normal and abnormal. Pavlov discovered classical conditioning, otherwise known as associative learning. Desensitizing can be called classical conditioning in action—a therapist can help a client work through a phobia or trauma through repeated exposure to the cause of the anxiety. E. L. Thorndike discovered operant conditioning, which relies on rewards and punishments to influence people's behavior. The most common current version of this therapy is cognitive-behavioral therapy, which focuses on both thoughts and behaviors of the patient.
- *Cognitive therapy.* This framework highlights what the patient thinks rather than what they do. Cognitive therapists believe that dysfunctional emotions or behaviors are a result of dysfunctional thinking. These practitioners seek to change their patients' thoughts and by so doing change how they feel and what they do.
- *Humanistic therapy.* This therapeutic approach focuses on a person's ability to make rational choices and develop to his/her maximum potential. Important themes in this framework include concern and respect for others. Key influences for this type of therapy include Jean-Paul Sartre, Martin Buber, and Soren Kierkegaard. There are three types of humanistic therapy that are especially influential: client-centered therapy, Gestalt therapy, and existential therapy.
- *Biological therapies.* This approach focuses on the biological causes of psychological disorders and seeks to eliminate or alleviate symptoms. Biological, or biomedical, therapies are often used in conjunction with psychotherapy. Many practitioners assert that biomedical approaches can enhance the effectiveness of other therapeutic approaches in many cases. The three primary forms of biomedical therapies are pharmacotherapy, or the use of medications in biomedical treatment; electroconvulsive therapy (ECT), or the use of electrical current in the brain; and psychosurgery, a type of neurosurgery in which a small piece of brain matter is destroyed or removed.

Antipsychotics

Antipsychotics are prescribed most often for the treatment of psychosis, such as in schizophrenia. Some side effects include drowsiness, restlessness, tremor, muscle spasms, dry mouth, and blurring of vision. A long-term side effect is tardive dyskinesia (TD), which is a disorder in which a person experiences involuntary movements most often in the mouth, lips, and tongue but sometimes other parts of the body. Typical antipsychotics include the following:

- Thorazine (chlorpromazine)
- Trilafon (perphenazine)
- Stelazine (trifluoperazine)
- Serentil (mesoridazine)
- Prolixin (fluphenazine)
- Navane (thiothixene)
- Moban (molindone)
- Mellaril (thioridazine)
- Loxitane (loxapine)
- Haldol (haloperidol)

There are also atypical antipsychotics whose side effects include dry mouth, blurred vision, constipation, dizziness, lightheadedness, and weight gain. They also sometimes can cause problems sleeping, fatigue, and weakness. Some atypical antipsychotics also have the long-term side effect of TD. Atypical antipsychotics include the following:

- Abilify (aripiprazole)
- Clozaril (clozapine)
- Geodon (ziprasidone)
- Risperdal (risperidone)
- Seroquel (quetiapine)
- Zyprexa (olanzapine)

Antidepressants

Antidepressants are a large category of medications used to treat depression. There are several different types of antidepressants. Selective serotonin reuptake inhibitors (SSRIs) gradually increase the amount of the neurotransmitter serotonin in the brain. Side effects include nausea, diarrhea, insomnia, and fatigue. Examples of SSRIs include the following:

- Celexa (citalopram)
- Lexapro (escitalopram)
- Luvox (fluvoxamine)
- Paxil (paroxetine)
- Prozac (fluoxetine)
- Zoloft (sertraline)

Another category of antidepressants are monoamine oxidase inhibitors (MAOIs). These are less common than SSRIs, and are used to treat complex, treatment-resistant depression. Side effects include dry mouth, headache, nausea, insomnia, dizziness, low blood pressure, sexual side effects, and weight gain. Some examples of MAOIs include the following:

- Emsam (selegiline)
- Marplan (isocarboxazid)
- Nardil (phenelzine)
- Parnate (tranylcypromine)

Tricyclics (TCAs) are another type of antidepressant that isn't used much currently. Their side effects include a drop in blood pressure, sedation, dry mouth, blurred vision, dizziness, and weight gain. Some examples include the following:

- Anafranil (clomipramine)
- Asendin (amoxapine)
- Elavil (amitriptyline)
- Norpramin (desipramine)
- Pamelor (nortriptyline)
- Sinequan (doxepin)
- Surmontil (trimipramine)
- Tofranil (imipramine)
- Vivactil (protriptyline)

Serotonin norepinephrine reuptake inhibitors (SNRIs) are another type of antidepressant that works by slowly increasing the amount of norepinephrine in the brain. Side effects include nausea, somnolence, constipation, dry mouth, dizziness, nervousness, increased heart rate, hypertension, and sexual dysfunction. Examples include the following:

- Pristiq (desvenlafaxine)
- Effexor (venlafaxine)
- Cymbalta (duloxetine)

Anti-Anxiety Medications

Anti-anxiety medications are used to treat numerous chronic and acute anxiety issues. One type of these medications is benzodiazepines. Also known as tranquilizers, they work quickly and can be effective for panic attacks. They can be quite physically addictive and are not recommended for long-term treatment. Side effects of benzodiazepines include drowsiness, dizziness, poor balance and coordination, slurred speech, difficulty concentrating and memory problems, confusion, stomach upset, headache, and blurred vision. Examples of benzodiazepines include the following:

- Xanax (alprazolam)
- Klonopin (clonazepam)
- Valium (diazepam)
- Ativan (lorazepam)
- Librium (chlordiazepoxide)
- Serax (oxazepam)
- Tranxene (clorazepate)

Buspirone (BuSpar) is another, newer anti-anxiety medication that also acts as a mild tranquilizer. Buspirone is slower acting than benzodiazepines but is not as sedating and does not impair memory and coordination. It seems to work well for generalized anxiety disorder but not other types of anxiety disorders. Side effects include nausea, headaches, dizziness, drowsiness, weight gain, upset stomach, nervousness, constipation/diarrhea, and dry mouth.

Beta blockers are often used to treat the physical symptoms of anxiety, especially social anxiety. They are used to control rapid heartbeat, shaking, trembling, and blushing for several hours. They are generally safe for most patients and have few side effects; however, they sometimes cannot treat stronger symptoms enough to cause relief. They do lower blood pressure and slow heart rate. Examples of beta blockers used for anxiety are Inderal (propranolol) and Tenormin (atenolol).

Stimulants

Stimulants are typically prescribed to individuals with attention deficit hyperactivity (ADHD) as they help regulate disorganized thought processes. Side effects include appetite loss, sleep problems, and mood swings. Examples include the following:

- Adderall (amphetamine and dextroamphetamine)
- Dexedrine (dextroamphetamine)
- Ritalin (methylphenidate)
- Strattera (atomoxetine)
- Focalin (dexmethylphenidate)
- Vyvanse (lisdexamfetamine)

Mood Stabilizers

Mood stabilizers are a type of psychotropic medication that are typically used to treat intense, repeated shifts in a person's mood. They are commonly used for patients experiencing bipolar, schizophrenia, or borderline personality. Mood stabilizers help balance neurotransmitters in the brain, which control emotional states and behavior. They can be used to treat mania and to prevent a return of both manic and depressive episodes. Some of these medications are known as anticonvulsants as they are also used to treat some types of seizures. Side effects include nausea and stomach upset, trembling, increased thirst, weight gain, and drowsiness. Examples of mood stabilizers include the following:

- Lithium
- Lamictal (lamotrigine)
- Tegretol or Equetro (carbamazepine)
- Depakote (valproic acid)

Types of Mental Health Professionals

Types of mental health professionals work with people dealing with psychological disorders and other mental health problems.

A psychiatrist is a medical doctor and is the only mental health professional who can prescribe medications (other than some psychiatric nurses). Other doctors also prescribe medications for mental health diagnoses, but they do not have specialized training in mental health. Most psychiatrists focus their practice on finding and prescribing the best medications to help their patients. There are a few who do psychotherapy as well.

Psychologists have a doctorate degree but are not medical doctors. Their degrees are usually either a PhD or a PsyD. PhD programs focus on either clinical or research work, and the amount of clinical experience a given psychologist has can vary greatly from program to program. In contrast, PsyD programs usually focus on clinical practice, and a psychologist with this degree will likely have thousands of hours of clinical experience before entering practice. Beyond clinical training and research, psychologists receive training in psychological assessment, diagnosis, and a wide variety of psychotherapies.

A clinical social worker has completed a master's degree in social work (MSW) program and may also carry the Licensed Clinical Social Worker (LCSW) designation, particularly if he/she is doing psychotherapy. MSW programs focus on direct work with clients and give their students many opportunities to do fieldwork. Requirements for LCSW certification require thousands of hours of direct clinical experience and passing a licensure exam.

Generally, psychiatric nurses first train to be a registered nurse (RN) and then go on to get specialized training in psychiatry and some forms of psychotherapy. They generally get up to 500 hours of direct clinical experience during their training. In many states psychiatric nurses also carry prescription privileges, and they can prescribe the same types of medications that a psychiatrist can.

Marriage and family therapists usually have a master's degree, although not all states require this. They generally have hundreds to thousands of hours of direct clinical experience. This designation varies widely from state to state; therefore, the quality of the work by each practitioner may also vary significantly from person to person.

A Licensed Professional Counselor (LPC) has completed a master's or doctoral degree and is trained to work with individuals and groups in the mental health field. Like MSWs their program focuses on direct work with clients, and they have many opportunities to do fieldwork. They must complete at least 3,000 hours of post-degree supervised clinical experience and pass a licensure exam. In some states they are referred to as licensed clinical professional counselors or licensed mental health counselors.

Issues Around Confidentiality

The American Psychological Association's code of ethics affirms that psychologists (and other mental health professionals) may share only the minimum information necessary when disclosing information. Additionally, practitioners should have express, written permission to share any information. Confidentiality is not unlimited, however. The law requires practitioners to report information in specific situations. Examples of these situations include the following:

- Receiving a court order
- To report ongoing domestic violence or to report any abuse or neglect of children, the elderly, or persons with disabilities
- To protect the patient or the public from serious harm—in cases in which a client discusses plans to harm themselves or another person

This last example refers to a practitioner's duty to warn, which is the responsibility to inform third parties or authorities of a threat (either to the client him/herself or to another person). Two important legal cases established the obligation of therapists to breach confidentiality in case a client poses a risk to self or others. The first is *Tarasoff v. Regents of the University of California*, in which a therapist did not inform a young woman and her parents of specific death threats that a client made against her. The therapist did inform police that the client posed a danger to himself and others, but the person against whom he made the threat was not warned, and he eventually murdered her. The courts ultimately ruled that confidentiality is trumped by the need for public safety.

The second case is that of Jablonski by *Pahls v. the United States*. This case further extended the responsibilities of duty to warn. A review of records for previous violent behavior was deemed necessary for a complete risk assessment. In this case a doctor conducted an assessment of a potentially violent client but did not review the client's history of violence. As a result, another person, a girlfriend, was not warned about the client's history of violent behavior. The client murdered the girlfriend.

Duty to warn gives therapists and other counselors both the obligation and the right to breach confidentiality if they believe a client poses a risk to another person. The therapist is protected from prosecution for breach of confidentiality if he/she made the breach in good faith and had reasonable suspicion that the client might be a danger to self or others.

Anthropology

Anthropology and General Anthropology

Anthropology is the study of all aspects of humankind and its immediate ancestors. It emphasizes a historical, comparative, and holistic approach. **General anthropology** considers the past, present, and future, as well as the biological, societal, cultural, and linguistic influences. Anthropology studies the ways in which humans adapt and change over time as a result of these different influences. General anthropology refers to the academic field of anthropology, which is subdivided into four primary areas: physical (or biological) anthropology, cultural (or socio-cultural) anthropology, linguistics, and archaeology. The scientific discipline of general anthropology began in the nineteenth century and was sparked in large part by interest in the origins of Native Americans.

Cultural Anthropology

Cultural anthropology is the description, analysis and interpretation of societal and cultural similarities and differences. **Cultural anthropology** is approached in two ways. The first is **ethnography** or fieldwork in a specific cultural setting. Data is collected from interaction with a particular community or group, often in poor and remote areas. The data is often presented descriptively, such as in a paper, book, or film. The other approach is **ethnology**, in which the investigator uses many data sources to look at differences and similarities across cultures and thus synthesize generalizations about society and culture. The ethnologist may use ethnography, archeological data, and/or other sources to develop these theories.

Archaeological Anthropology

Archaeological anthropology or **archaeology** is the study of ancient cultures through examination of material remains. These remains give insight into the behavior and cultural patterns of these earlier humans. Archeologists collect **artifacts** such as tools, earthenware, parts of old buildings, garbage, and plant and animal remains. The artifacts and the relationships between them are useful for reconstructing a vision of a previous culture. They often excavate or dig through levels of areas to glean changes over time. Another methodology is the examination of the **paleoecology** or relationship between living things in an area. Archeologists also sometimes study more recent or even contemporary cultures by analyzing their material remains which give information that may differ from written or verbal communications.

Physical Anthropology

Physical anthropology (also known as **biological anthropology**) is the analysis of human biological diversity over time and space. The discipline encompasses five areas of *human variation*: human paleoanthropology or evolution as evidenced by fossil records, human genetics, human growth and progression, biological plasticity or capacity for change under stress, and the study of nonhuman primates. **Physical anthropology** is intrinsically connected to other disciplines, notably biological and medical fields as well as archeology. Both genetics and environmental influences are considered in the analysis of temporal and spatial human diversity.

Linguistic Anthropology

Linguistic anthropology or **linguistics** is the analysis of language diversity over time and space within a societal or cultural framework. Generalizations about language are sometimes made based on these analyses. Some linguists use modern languages to recreate ancient ones and gain historical perspective. Because language is closely tied to other cultural influences, linguistic and cultural anthropologists often work together to relate linguistic differences to cultural perceptions over time. **Sociolinguistics** is the study of relationships between language and societal factors such as class, ethnicity, or geography.

Connection of Anthropology to Science and Humanities

Strictly speaking, anthropology is a **science** because it uses systematic principles, experimentation, observation, and logic in context to the material and physical world. It utilizes many of the natural sciences as well as the social sciences. The natural science connections include geology, zoology, chemistry and others. There are many similarities and overlaps between anthropology and the social sciences of sociology and psychology. Since anthropology is holistic, it is also deeply connected to fields in the **humanities** such as language studies, literature, philosophy, folklore, and the arts.

Anthropology and Archeology

Applied anthropology is the use of anthropological information, theories and techniques to address contemporary problems. Applied anthropologists are often employed in medical fields like public health or family planning, forensics, business or economic growth, or cultural resource management. **Cultural resource management (CRM)** is a common mode of applied or public archeology. CRM involves making decisions about preservation and selective destruction of portions of sites. Cultural resource managers are often hired by governmental agencies and may work in conjunction with applied cultural anthropologists. Applied archeologists may also work in the field of historic preservation or develop educational programs for the public.

Hypothesis, Theory, and Association

A hypothesis is a tentative but as yet unconfirmed explanation for a relationship. It suggests a possible but unproven reason for an **association**, which is an observed connection between two or more variables. The **hypothesis** provides a tentative explanation of the impact of changes in a predictor or independent variable on another dependent variable (also called the explicandum). The hypothesis must be tested using scientific methods before a **theory** can be developed to explain the nature of the associations. These scientific methods include random case selection, reliable measurements, and use of proper statistical techniques for analysis. A theory should be verifiable through later research.

Stages of Scientific Method in Anthropology

First, a research question is posed. A hypothesis or tentative explanation of a relationship is developed, usually based on an observed association. A mechanism to explain the hypothesis is put forward. Information relevant to the hypothesis is gathered using random sampling of cross-cultural data. A quantifiable or coded means of measuring data points must be established. The data is then analyzed by looking for patterns or associations and using suitable statistical methods to appraise the intensity of the associations. Based on the data analysis, the original hypothesis is confirmed or other conclusions are drawn. Other inferences may be speculated based on the conclusions. A theory or verifiable explanation is developed or a previous theory is supported.

Use of Multiple Variables

Many research studies are designed to test the association between one **predictor** or **independent variable** and one **dependent variable**. In other instances, it is appropriate to look at a number of potential predictor variables, all or any of which may have effects upon or be correlated to the dependent variable. Predictor variables can be studied for their influence on the dependent variable separately or in some combination. Use of **multiple variables** can make it difficult to differentiate between a statistical correlation, a high relatedness of variables, and a true cause and effect relationship in which a change in the predictor variable genuinely influences a result in the dependent variable.

Development Anthropology Entails

Development anthropology is a field of applied anthropology concerned with social and cultural issues in the context of economic development. People in this field design and help to implement policies. These policies are generally directed toward increased equity, a reduction of poverty, and a more equitable allocation of wealth. Strategies for economic change that are compatible with the local culture and economic structure have been found to be most successful. Policies that attempt to over-innovate or accomplish too much change, as well as those that under-differentiate or disregard local cultural diversity, tend to fail.

Anthropology and Education

Anthropology and education is a branch of applied anthropology in which students are studied within the framework of their family, cohorts, and enculturation. **Enculturation** refers to the socialization process for learning about culture and passing it on across generations. In most of these types of studies, students are observed in classroom or community settings to see how they relate to each other, teachers, and/or others. Strategies for improving learning are often implemented, taking into account language and cultural differences between various students. This is often done in conjunction with a sociolinguist.

Urban Anthropology

Urban anthropology is the analysis of cities and urban life. Basic theoretical research and applied anthropology are both done in this field. **Urban anthropologists** deal with issues like distinguishing major social groups in the urban context, aiding urban migrants in those groups in their dealings with various services, and urban violence. Since the time of the Industrial Revolution, the percentage of people living in cities has grown to about 50% today and is increasing. The social and cultural distinctions between urban and rural dwellers are diminishing as there is increased migration and travel between the two. While less-developed countries currently have a lower percentage of city dwellers, their urbanization growth rate is higher than in developed countries.

Medical Anthropology

The field of medical anthropology is concerned with studying diseases and illnesses in different populations, the influence of social constructs on illness, and health-care systems in various contexts. **Medical anthropologists** come from all four sub-disciplines of anthropology and perform both theoretical research and applied functions. **Disease** is a health threat caused by a defined genetic cause or pathogen whereas illness is any state perceived by a person to be poor health. **Illness** is defined often by cultural views. Social constructs affecting disease rates include things like religious beliefs, the degree of cultural isolation, and cultural practices. Contemporary medical anthropologists perform functions like providing cultural context in public health programs and examining issues about the definition of life and personhood (for example, stem cell research and extraordinary measures to prolong life).

Distinctions Between Major Health-Care Systems

Health-care systems are the principles, customs, and individuals involved in preventing and curing illnesses. Various cultures approach **health-care systems** through one of three theories as to the origins of illness: personalistic, emotionalistic, or naturalistic. According to **personalistic disease theories**, the source of illness is some sort of mediator like a witch or ghost. **Emotionalistic disease theories** presume that illnesses develop from various emotional states. Western medicine or biomedicine is an example of the third type, **naturalistic disease theories** that explain illnesses on an impersonal level based on scientific principles or some defined change. The health-care system prevalent in a culture indicates the most likely curer people will employ for diagnosis and treatment. Those who believe in personalistic theories may use a shaman whereas those valuing naturalistic theories usually employ a medical doctor. There is also a distinction between Western systems, which generally completely separate biological and psychological origins of illness, and non-Western systems, which tend to be more holistic and less rigid in their distinctions.

Anthropology in Business Applications

Cultural anthropologists are often hired for **business applications**. Ethnography and the techniques of observation are utilized to collect data. The anthropologist's cross-cultural expertise and awareness of cultural differences are useful to companies. For example, the company may want to improve relationships between managers and workers within the sphere of their group. A company may wish to find ways to improve the design of superior products and improve sales to defined audiences. Anthropologists can aid an organization in developing marketing techniques that are culturally appropriate in different marketplaces.

Systematic Survey

A systematic or **field survey** is one of the two fundamental types of field work, the other being *excavation*. **Paleoanthropologists**, who look for fossils or remains of ancient hominid and later human life, generally work in tandem with archaeologists, who concentrate on material remains such as tools, building remnants, and other artifacts. A systematic survey is an examination of settlement patterns from a regional perspective. A **settlement pattern** is the scattering of sites in a specific region. The surveyor walks around the entire region if possible (or uses some remote sensing), logs the locations and dimensions of sites, and approximates the date of occupation of each based on surface artifacts found. The relationships between sites can be used to infer lifestyle (for example, hunters) and social complexity.

Excavations

Excavations are field work in which layers of earth or the *stratigraphies* are dug through at a site. It is assumed that older layers or *strata* are on the bottom, successive layers are newer as they get to the surface, and remains found in a particular layer are from that time period. **Excavation** requires a good deal of physical labor and financial resources. Generally, only sites that are threatened or that can be useful from a research perspective are excavated. Permission and informed consent from governmental or other agencies in charge of protection of the site is often needed before an excavation may be started. Some countries expect preliminary archaeological impact studies before any actual field work is done.

<u>Process</u>

Initially, a **grid** is used to divide the surface into equal sections or collection units. Surface materials are gathered and their exact location is documented three-dimensionally. Using this information, the sections with greatest potential are dug. There are two ways to dig. The first is generally used for test pits and is relatively fast. It involves removing everything to a particular depth in a collection unit. An example is **test boring** in which a narrow column of soil is removed, generally using a hollow metal tube. The other method is to tunnel through layer by layer, looking for and collecting fossils and artifacts in each. Soil is generally put through a screen to recover small or broken remains. A procedure called **flotation** is typically utilized. In flotation, water is used to dissolve the soil which is then put through several fine meshes for sorting. Carbonized plant materials drift to the top and heavier vestiges like bones sink to the bottom.

Forces That Influence Taphonomy

Taphonomy is the analysis of processes that have an effect on the remains of dead animals. It is tied closely to **fossilization** or the preservation of remains. For example, body components that are hard – such as bones or dentition – are more likely to be preserved that soft parts like skin. Vestiges that were buried in lighter, freshly formed types of sediments such as silt or sand are also more liable to be preserved. Thus, sediments from caves and other wet areas like flood plains, lakes, volcanic ash, and valleys or basins are good sources of fossils. The pH of the sediment can affect the degree of preservation as acid causes even harder tissues to disintegrate. Fossils are more likely to be found in drier areas than wet ones. All of these forces combine to bias our views of prior animal and human activity and where it occurred.

Lower Paleolithic Tools

The **Paleolithic** or **Old Stone Age** occurred approximately 750,000 until 15,000 years ago. It is divided into three periods, each related to junctures of human evolution. *Homo erectus* lived during the earliest **Lower Paleolithic**, archaic *Homo sapiens* species lived during the **Middle Paleolithic**, and anatomically modern humans lived during the **Upper Paleolithic**. Each time period also produced characteristic tool-making traditions. Stone tools from the Lower Paleolithic subdivision are termed **Acheulian tools**. They appear to have evolved from earlier pebble or **Oldowan tools** (discussed further elsewhere). The major distinctions between Oldowan and Acheulian tools were the increasing complexity of and greater use of flakes to make tools in the latter. Both traditions relied heavily on the hand ax, a core of rock chipped off using a smaller flat piece called a flake. Whereas Oldowan tools usually were just chipped off somewhat at one end, the Acheulian tools were chipped all over to make a flat, oval ax with an improved cutting surface. Other Acheulian tools included chisel-like tools called burins and some scrapers.

Middle Paleolithic Tools

Middle Paleolithic or **Middle Stone Age** tools are associated with archaic species of *Homo sapiens*, in particular the Neanderthals. This age extended from approximately 250,000 to 40,000 years ago. The Neanderthals worked in the **Mousterian tool-making tradition**, which included a minimum of fourteen types of tools for specific jobs, and used highly-developed modifications of the **Levallois technique**. They used this technique to whittle off flakes from a special core of rock and then refined the tools for specific purposes. They had several types of scrapers for preparing animal hides, other tools for sawing, and others to make holes or slices.

Upper Paleolithic Tools

The Upper Paleolithic or **Late Stone Age** in Europe and Africa respectively extended from approximately 40,000 to 10,000 years ago and is connected to the emergence of anatomically modern humans. There were several tool-making traditions during the Middle Stone Age. In succession, they were the *Aurignacian, Gravettian, Solutrean,* and *Magdelanian*. Upper Paleolithic or Late Stone Age tools generally associated with anatomically modern humans were notable for their blade-making techniques, which became increasingly delicate and intricate. The **Solutrean tradition** produced projectile points like arrowheads, and the **Magdelanian** is known for development of small, sharp micro blades that could be set into handles made of other materials. A blade tool was created from a core by chipping long (4 to 6 inch) blades off it using a punch made of antler or bone and a hammerstone. Upper Paleolithic tools were increasingly specialized and diverse depending on the region and ancestral traditions. Implements found include needles with eyes (suggesting sewing of clothes) and fishhooks (indicating fishing). .

Differences Between Middle and Upper Paleolithic Ages

A number of changes occurred during the **transition** from the Middle to Upper Paleolithic (Middle to Late Stone) ages. Increasing specialization and refinement of tool making is discussed elsewhere. In addition, bones, ivory, and antlers were used in conjunction with stone for tools. The first evidence of the manufacture of **non-utilitarian objects** such as jewelry is found during the Late Stone Age. Whereas Middle Paleolithic dwellers were primarily opportunistic hunters, during the Upper Paleolithic time period the survival base was broadened to include fishing, catching birds, trapping of small mammals, and big-game hunting. Some areas appear to have been more densely populated in the latter period. A far-reaching set of trade connections and presumably social assimilation developed as well, evidenced by findings of raw materials far from their origin. The Upper Paleolithic people developed elaborate **burials** and placed personal items with the buried corpses. They also were the first known group to create works of art (see another card for further discussion).

Cave Paintings from the European Upper Paleolithic Age

Several hundred caves containing **paintings** from the Upper Paleolithic Age exist in southwestern France and northern Spain. In general, the paintings are mature, fluid, multi-dimensional, and natural depictions of **animals**. The artists used **natural pigments** ground into powders and then blended with a **binding agent** like grease or blood. They applied the paint to the cave walls using their fingers, wooden spatulas, or rudimentary brushes. The reasons for painting primarily animals are unclear, but the animals depicted are generally specific to the region, and often bones of these animals are found in close proximity. The animals and their relationships may reflect some magical significance, the role they played in the human's existence, or the fear associated with certain animals. For some reason, these cave paintings usually have some simple geometric patterns as well. Human beings are rarely depicted, but handprints are more common.

Artistic Expressions from the European Upper Paleolithic Age

Artists from the European Upper Paleolithic Age produced many carvings and engravings. They were either naturalistic renderings of animals or some type of fusion of animal and human. Cave painting renderings of animal-humans are also found. The significance of these **hybrid carvings** may be related to spiritual beliefs. There is also limited evidence that some of the carvings had rudimentary **scientific origins**, such as an antler found in France that appears to have a short lunar calendar on it. Another prevalent artistic expression was **Venus figurines** or sculptures of women

- 102 -

in limestone, ivory, or clay. The women were usually depicted faceless. There was a range of sizes and shapes represented, but some are anatomically unusual with overstated secondary sexual characteristics.

Archaeology of the Early Australians

Australia represents a unique niche because the continent was inaccessible other than by water for more than 30 million years. In actuality, a landmass called **Sahul** or **Greater Australia**, which also incorporated the current New Guinea and Tasmania, was formed during the **Pleistocene era**. The most convincing time period for human settlement of Australia is 40,000 years ago, although some findings suggest earlier habitation. There were either several waves of immigration, with the last being a robust population ancestral to modern aborigines, or early gracile migrants evolved into more robust variants. The earliest remains have been found along the coasts, lakes, or river beds. Stone tools and equipment related to use of fire have been discovered at various places. Artifacts from the dry interior regions are dated later, starting approximately 26,000 years ago.

Archaeology Artifacts from Upper Paleolithic Age in the Americas

At present, there is still debate as to whether the **Americas** were originally settled possibly as far back as 50,000 years ago by various groups, or the more popular view that the original migration was 13,000 to 12,000 years ago by **Late Pleistocene Asians**. During several of the glacial periods, the sea level subsided enough to create the **Beringia** or **Bering Land Bridge** connecting northeastern Asia and northwestern North America. In particular, the Bridge was uncovered for the entire period of time from 35,000 to 11,000 years ago. Similarities between tools found in Siberia and Alaska suggest the former as the most likely origin of the migration. Alaskan archaeological sites have unearthed tools dated as far back as 11,800 years ago, but earlier migration is suggested by findings such as those in Meadowcroft Rockshelter near Pittsburgh dated earlier than 12,800 years ago, Monte Verde in Chile at 13,000 years old, and others possibly even older.

First Americans and Paleo-Indians

The first Americans are difficult to classify, which places their origin in contention. The oldest skeletons discovered, which at this point are comparatively few, do not resemble what is expected based on modern Native Americans or northeast Asians. On average, the early American skulls are longer and the faces thinner. However, this does not necessarily disprove theories about early Asian migration or the connection of Native Americans to earlier inhabitants because many years and opportunities for evolution separate each. Analysis of mitochondrial DNA does show five common **haplogroups** or **biological lineages** shared by Native Americans and northeast Asians. It is clear that there was a group of New World people termed **Paleo-Indians** who thrived around 12,000 to 10,000 years ago. There were hunters (especially of big game) and their tools included sophisticated fluted points that could be attached to a pole. They were also gatherers of fruit. These Paleo-Indians spread pretty much all over North America and then South America. They adapted to various environments including the plains and tropical rain forests.

Mesolithic Tools

The Mesolithic or **Middle Stone Age** came after the Upper Paleolithic Age and is associated with anatomically modern humans. The distinguishing feature of tools during this time period is that they were generally **microliths**, which are very small and usually triangular flints. In Europe, this tradition appears to have started around 12,000 years ago and peaking about 10,000 years ago when glaciers had withdrawn significantly. This lusher environment enabled the people to do

- 103 -

solitary hunting and trapping and to fish more extensively. In Europe, microliths found from this period include specialized tools like fishhooks, harpoons, arrows, and new versions of axes and other traditional tools. **Woodworking techniques** were upgraded, evidenced by things like dugout canoes and bows. In more tropical regions in Africa and Asia, tools from this time reflect the greater emphasis on **gathering** in those areas.

Mesolithic and Other Archaic Cultures of the Early Holocene Epoch

The Holocene epoch is the modern one we continue to live in. It began roughly 10,000 to 11,000 years ago when there was a retreat of the glaciers and a broad warming worldwide. The anatomically modern humans at this time generally became more sedentary. In Europe, the beginning of the **Holocene** is associated with **Mesolithic people**. They derived their subsistence from a much broader range of sources than before because of the shift to a warmer and more verdant environment. They were foragers, indicating that they took advantage of any suitable food available including wild plants, wild animals, fish, shellfish, and birds. In North America, the **Archaic period** is dated slightly later, from about 9000 to 3000 years ago. Here, adaptations were more regional. For example, in the American southeast, freshwater shellfish were a main staple for food and the population is known as the Shell Mound Archaic people. Sites in the Midwest show a more diverse diet there including plants, nuts, fish, and shellfish. In Africa and the Middle East, evidence suggests that shifts toward more varied sources of sustenance occurred several thousand years earlier.

Shift from Hunting and Gathering to Food Production in the Middle East

Prior to about 15,000 years ago, the major source of sustenance in the **Middle East** (as well as most other places) was **big game**. The shift toward **foraging** for diverse plant and animal foods began earliest in the Middle East after glacial recession. From about 12,000 to 10,000 years ago, people in this area were primarily semi-nomadic hunters and gatherers. Beginning around 10,000 years ago, they started to domesticate plants like barley and wheat and animals such as goats and sheep. They did non-irrigated dry farming. Starting around 7500 years ago, food production became more specialized with addition of new produce and domestication of cattle and swine. By about 5500 years ago, agriculture was extensive in the region and some formal towns had been established.

Neolithic

Neolithic literally means the "New Stone Age" where polished stone tools and weapons were developed for use. However, the more important distinction of the **Neolithic Age** is that it was the first cultural stage in which human groups relied on domestication and agriculture for subsistence. Therefore, the Neolithic Age began at slightly different times in various regions. **Domestication** means the modification through artificial selection by humans of a wild plant or animal variety into a more useful form. **Agriculture** refers to the occupation of farming. The cultural shift toward a Neolithic economy permitted relatively rapid lifestyle changes.

Natufians

The Natufians were a pervasive Middle Eastern culture who lived approximately 12,500 to 10,500 years ago. They lived either in the subtropical woodland area called the Hilly Flanks or on its periphery. They were dependent on broad-spectrum foraging, gathering wild cereals, and hunting gazelles. This enabled them initially to develop a sedentary lifestyle and to live in early villages. Many experts believe that **Natufians** living in the more marginal regions such as Ali Kosh in the piedmont steppe were the first to begin **cultivation**. This is because around 11,000 years ago, the weather became drier, making it more difficult for those living in the less lush areas to readily forage. In order to maintain the lifestyle they were accustomed to (relatively sedentary village life), they needed to maintain communities near water sources and develop new survival strategies such as planting and harvesting of crops.

Regions and Vertical Economy of the Ancient Middle East

The ancient Middle East was a vertical economy. This means that the people took advantage of differing environmental zones that were in close proximity. Foragers could travel from one zone to another in order to exploit the game or wild plants available in a particular season. In the ancient Middle East, there were four environmental areas where foragers could travel to at various times of the year. The easternmost and highest was the **high plateau**, a source of pastureland. To the west of that, separated by mountains, was the **Hilly Flanks**, which was subtropical woodland with plentiful wild wheat and barley. This was bordered to the west by the **piedmont steppe** or treeless plain, a good region for winter as it was generally rainy and game animals grazed there. Adjacent to the southwestern section of the piedmont steppe was the **alluvial desert**. The alluvial desert was once thought to be the area were food production began as it has a number of rivers (Euphrates, Tigris, Karun) contributing to rich, fertile soil. Raw materials were also moved between areas, such as copper from the high plateau and asphalt from the piedmont steppe.

Wild and Domesticated Plants and Animals of the Ancient Middle East

In general, domesticated plants produce a bigger seed and higher yield than wild ones, but they also have changes that deter natural **seed distribution mechanisms**. In the ancient Middle East, the major **wild plants** were *cereals* like wheat and barley. They could disperse new seeds easily because their axes to where seeds were connected were brittle and broke off. **Domesticated** versions were specifically selected to have stronger connective tissues to retain the seeds on the stem as well as other features such as more easily broken husks. Generally, domestication of animals produced *smaller animals* that were easier to handle. Initially, the people domesticated sheep (to be woolly) and goats (horn differences) followed by other animals like pigs and cattle.

Neolithic Age in Africa

A minimum of **seven world areas** separately developed from the transition of foraging to cultivation. In addition to the Middle East, one of the earliest was in **Africa** near the **Nabta Playa basin** in southern Egypt. The region was settled about 12,000 years ago. By about 11,000 years ago, there were small camps used seasonally by domesticated cattle drivers. By approximately 9000 years ago, there were permanent villages, but they had not yet domesticated plants. However, within a few hundred years they were making some of the earliest pottery found in the region. There is archeological evidence that Nabta became a regional ceremonial center somewhere around 8000 years ago, suggesting great organization and social complexity. Other African Neolithic locations have also been documented. Nabta was resettled after a major drought about 7500 years ago, and the earliest evidence of domestication of plants was about 4000 years ago with sorghum, pearl millet, and African rice.

Neolithic Age in Europe and Asia

The shift from **foraging** to **cultivation** spread rapidly initially into Mediterranean areas and then through much of Europe and Asia starting around 8000 years ago. However, two regions in **China** are credited with the independent domestication of specific plants or animals. Two types of *millet* were domesticated in the harsh **Yellow River region** of northern China about 7500 years ago. Further south in China along the **Yangtze River**, *rice* was first domesticated a little earlier as well as

Copyright © Mometrix Media. You have been licensed one copy of this document for personal use only. Any other reproduction or redistribution is strictly prohibited. All rights reserved.

pigs, dogs, and water buffalo. There is evidence that rice may have been independently cultivated in other areas such as Thailand.

Clovis Tradition

The Clovis tradition was a short-lived, early American tool tradition of some Paleo-Indians. It is characterized by sophisticated **projectile points** that were attached to spears. The **Clovis tradition** was practiced at most for about 450 years around 12,000 years ago in the North American Central Plains and in the Eastern United States. Tools in other traditions dating from the same time period have been found in Wisconsin and earlier in Chile. These findings suggest that **migration** to the Americans may have occurred as early as 18,000 years ago, and genetic analysis bolsters the idea that the immigrants were of more than one haplogroup or ancestry.

Neolithic Age in the Americas

There are at least three regions in the Americas where **food cultivation** occurred separately. The first was **Mesoamerica** in Central America, which produced domesticated plants such as maize, beans, and squash and domesticated dogs and turkeys during the time period between 8000 and 4700 years ago. The **Andean region** of South America developed domesticated plants like squash, potato, beans, and quinoa as well as animals such as llama, alpaca, and guinea pigs all between 10,000 and 5000 years ago. Additionally, Native Americans in the **eastern United States** had independently cultivated a number of domesticated plants by about 4500 years ago, including squash and goosefoot which were used to complement what they could hunt and gather.

Evidence that New World Domestication Originated in Tropical Regions

Experts believe that **New World cultivation** originated in the tropical lowlands of **South America** and then extended to **Central America**, **Mexico**, and the **Caribbean**. Teams studying plant materials such as pollens, crystals (phytoliths), and starch grains of wild and domesticated squash and gourds put the origins of their farming at about 10,000 years ago in areas like Ecuador and Peru. Molecular genetic work indicates that maize was originally domesticated in the lowlands of southwestern Mexico and may have evolved from a wild grain called teosinte. Phytoliths indicate that maize farming had extended as far east as the Mexican Gulf Coast by about 7300 years ago. By approximately 3500 years ago, maize farms using pot irrigation and stable villages based on these endeavors were prevalent in the Valley of Oaxaca in the Mexican southern highlands.

Domestication of Plants and Animals and the Conversion to the Neolithic

Only fourteen animals and a small fraction of recognized plant species have been **domesticated**. The consistent theme is a movement toward a more **sedentary lifestyle** and its maintenance. During the **Neolithic Age**, the plants selected by the people for domestication depended on factors like availability, ease of domestication, and the need relative to other sources of food like animals that could be hunted or plants that could be foraged. The easiest species to cultivate are **self-pollinating plants** like wheat. Different animals were native to various regions and very few were easy to domesticate and adapt for the uses desired by the inhabitants. The wild animals most adaptable to taming were those that lived in **hierarchical flocks** like cattle because they were and are used to being subservient. Geography definitely played a role in the spread of farming, with areas allowing for easy migration to similar climates (such as across Eurasia) more likely to show rapid expansion. The cost/benefit ratio of food production also influenced development and spread (discussed further on another card).

Costs and Benefits Involved with Shift from Foraging to Food Production

Food production definitely requires more work than foraging. The diet of peoples who are primarily **food producers** is usually less varied and nutritious than that of foragers. This can lead to a greater prevalence of **communicable diseases** and other **public health problems**. Whereas foragers operated on a basis of equality, the more sedentary food producers developed property divisions, created forms of bondage like slavery, committed more crimes and war, and polluted and degraded the environment. On the other hand, the shift toward food production and sedentariness allowed for more consistent crop yields, development of new inventions, novel political and social structures, scientific and creative advancements, the development of written languages, economic advancements, and urban life in general.

Non-Invasive Techniques for Archaeological Examination of Sites

Archaeological sites are areas with evidence of previous human presence as indicated by human artifacts and/or features. A feature is any fixed remain indicative of prior human activity such as a fireplace or grave. Field or systematic surveys of archaeological sites are noninvasive (unlike excavation). Any technique that uses equipment that does not actually remove soil is considered remote sensing. Examples of remote sensing techniques include electrical resistivity surveying, proton magnetometry, ground penetrating radar (GPR), and satellite photographs. Electrical resistivity surveying utilizes an electrical current which is delivered through the ground; differences in electrical resistance suggest the presence of artifacts or features. In proton magnetometry, a meter gauges the intensity of the earth's magnetic field on the surface with variations, again indicating possible artifacts or elements. GPR uses a radar signal from above the surface to send an electromagnetic pulse into the soil; if there are any archeological remains or other objects, the pulse will echo back off of them.

Random and Representative Samples

Archaeological sites are often studied by taking random and representative samples of the site. Both should be collected without preconceived notions of the important areas of the site. **Random sampling** involves taking soil samples from arbitrarily selected points throughout the research area. The goal here is to find **representative samples**. Common sampling approaches are to transect or make a line of equally spaced test borings or to set up a grid for similar borings. A representative sample is a smaller sample that proportionately typifies the larger population in terms of important characteristics such as the age and size of samples, the activities represented, the functions of the artifacts, and human remains found.

Important Considerations During Excavation

Excavation of an archaeological site usually involves dividing the site into **grids** and then digging **excavation units**. The researcher scrapes down and identifies units either by changes in soil characteristics or by using consistent increments. Each is sifted through a screen to capture every possible artifact. Valid excavation should maintain the **spatial context** or relationship between all artifacts in different excavation units. The **provenience** or exact location of an artifact should be documented along with the spatial relationships or associations between all objects found. The most ideal way to maintain all of these factors is to leave the artifacts in place and label them. Some sort of permanent documentation should be done such as photographing them in place or diagramming them in spatial context.

Ethnography and Related Fields

Ethnography is the rigorous analysis and description of a specific culture by direct interaction with them. **Paleoethnography** is the reconstruction of a previous cultural structure by examining archaeological remains. **Ethnoarchaeology** is the study of existing populations to gain knowledge about how archaeological evidence is produced. Former cultures can be reconstructed using these types of studies to form an **ethnographic analogy** in which written modern-day or historical records provide a context for interpretation of archeological data. An example of this is a **direct historical methodology** in which historical ethnographic reports from actual descendants of ancient cultural groups are utilized to gain insight about the earlier culture. Other ways to reconstruct a past culture include actual reproduction of artifacts or portions of a site, analysis of wear patterns on tools, and using various methodologies to look at the former environment, diet, social structure, trade patterns and/or ideologies (discussed further elsewhere).

Methods of Reconstructing Ancient Environmental Conditions

Overall **climate changes** are usually reconstructed by examining the ratio between two oxygen isotopes ($^{16}O:^{18}O$) in the ancient exoskeletons of microscopic marine organisms called **foraminifera**. This information is useful because foraminifera integrate oxygen from seawater into their skeletons. ^{16}O is a lighter oxygen isotope than ^{18}O. During warmer phases, seawater evaporates but returns to the ocean as rain, maintaining a constant isotope ratio. However, during colder climatic periods, some of the water evaporated from the sea becomes snow instead and does not go back into the sea, reducing the relative amount of ^{16}O and the $^{16}O:^{18}O$ ratio. Another method is to look at preserved pollen remains, a field called **palynology**, as certain plant species tend to thrive under specific environmental conditions.

Studying Ancient Diets to Gain Insight into Cultures

Often, **food remains** can be found directly at archaeological sites at hearths or trash piles. They are generally separated using flotation methods and then identified by comparison using other bones, seeds, or nuts. Examination of **animal carcasses** is utilized to gain insight into hunting practices or ritualistic use of animals. Wear patterns on the **dentition** of the humans can suggest their diet. Examination of human **bones** can provide information about dietary deficiencies and composition. For example, carbon isotope analysis comparing the $^{12}C:^{13}C$ ratio in bones can indicate the types of plants in the diet. **Plants** that were in the region can be identified by examining phytoliths or microscopic, species-specific, opal silica bodies. In dry places where organic materials are better preserved, prehistoric **feces** (termed paleofeces or coprolites) can be analyzed.

Methods of Reconstructing the Social Structure and Ideology of Ancient Cultures

The social structure of an ancient culture is principally the pattern of marriage and living arrangements. By studying the **postmarital residence pattern** or place where married couples lived, ancient societies can be typed as primarily **matrilocal** or **patrilocal**. This means the married couple lived with either the wife's or husband's family. Social systems can often be inferred by looking at all archaeological remains. For example, if artifacts typically made or used by women or men (such as pottery or spearheads) are found only in certain areas, the postmarital pattern can be ascertained. The ideology or belief system of a culture can be inferred by looking at things like burial practices.

Techniques for Determining Trade Patterns of Ancient Peoples

Trade patterns can be ascertained by analyzing artifacts to determine the original source of **raw materials**. Three of the most commonly used techniques are petrographic analysis, trace element analysis, and neutron activation analysis. In **petrographic analysis**, slivers of rock are removed from a stone artifact and inspected microscopically. If the morphology observed matches other known rock sources, the origin can be traced. **Trace element analysis** is based on the observation that many materials have small or trace amounts of other elements characteristic of the region of origin. **Neutron activation analysis** is a highly-sensitive type of trace element analysis for chemical characterization of raw materials.

Use of Comparative Osteology to Identify Species

Comparative osteology is the study of bones of diverse species to look for similarities and differences. **Species** of animals are categorized based on similar looks and behaviors. Animals that look similar may be classified into the same genus, but if they cannot interbreed and produce fertile offspring they are considered different species. Fossil remains of ancient animals and humans that no longer exist only provide information about **skeletal morphology** (and even that may be sketchy), not behavioral patterns or reproductive ability. Therefore, traditionally the only basis for species identification was a comparison of bone morphology. Luckily, present day anthropologists have other identification tools at their disposal such as DNA analysis of bone remains.

Methods of Determining Sex of Specimens

On average, human beings as well as many other animals show **sexual dimorphism** or distinctive features for male and female. Males are usually bigger and more muscular than females. For humans and their ancestors, the two main skeletal areas used for sex classification are the skull and pelvis, which together provide correct identification in approximately 98% of cases. For primates including humans, the male skull generally has a smaller jaw angle, squarer chin, heavier musculature, more developed brow ridges, and bigger mastoids than the female, and they have an external occipital protuberance which is missing in the female. The three main differences between the pelvises are that a female generally has an outward splayed ilia, a wider greater sciatic notch, and a bigger subpubic angle. The major issues with these types of methods are that averages do not necessarily apply to a particular specimen, and it is unknown whether sexual dimorphism always existed.

Methods of Determining Age at Death of Specimens

There are certain characteristic features that can be used to approximate **age at death** of a specimen. The **dentition pattern** is helpful, as individual baby or deciduous teeth as well as permanent teeth generally erupt at a certain age. Another informative technique is to look at the pattern of **cranial suture closure**. Sutures are lines of attachment between cranial bones. An infant has soft areas between bones of the skull until these various sutures are filled in with more bone. The filling generally occurs in a regular, predictable pattern at a specific age, the last being the basilar suture at twenty-five years of age. A fairly good aging technique is to look at the pattern of **epiphyseal union**. There are characteristic ages when the central shaft or diaphysis of a particular skeletal bone fuses permanently to the end caps or epiphyses through ossification of the cartilage. The way in which the two halves of the pelvis are joined at the pubis (the pubis symphysis) starts changing around age eighteen, possibly providing information about age at death.

Ascertaining Information from Skeletons of Specimens

<u>Health and Behavior</u>

Information about a specimen's **health at death** can be ascertained by looking at the skeleton. Various **diseases** leave distinctive signs on the skeleton such as lesions in certain areas. **Development abnormalities** (such as spine curvature), fractures, wounds, and trephining are readily obvious on the skeleton. **Trephining** is a primitive surgical procedure in which big holes were bored into the skull to theoretically cure an illness. Childhood **malnutrition** is indicated by growth arrest lines, horizontal fissures toward the end of long bones, or enamel hypoplasia in adults. The appearance of **enamel hypoplasia** is the pitting and cracking of tooth enamel. The skeleton can reveal information about behavior practices such as Native American use of cradleboards to carry babies, which flattened both the forehead and posterior of the skull.

<u>Appearance</u>

Possible appearance can be extrapolated from skeletal remains based on several assumptions. Certain individual bones are indicative of overall **height**. Bone size is directly related to **musculature and build**. Particular **genetic features** like eye or nose shape or dentition and anatomical relationships such as the ratio of arm to leg length are more likely to be found in certain geographic regions. **Cranial features** are particularly characteristic of different species and often geographical areas; these include things like size of brain, shape of chin, amount of postorbital constriction, and the extent of the brow ridge or forehead. Missing areas of the skull are often filled in to make an endocast, or features are added to reconstruct a possible appearance generally based on assumptions from modern-day humans.

Hypotheses About Origins of Agriculture Based on Development of Sedentary Lifestyle

The **oasis hypothesis** of Childe theorized that early inhabitants gathered in oases, fertile areas fed by underground springs, fostering a more stationary and sedentary lifestyle. This eventually led to domestication of plants and animals. Carl Sauer espoused the **sedentary hypothesis**, which put forth that domestication started in places where the soil was rich but not flooded and people were already fairly sedentary, allowing them time for experimentation. The **marginal habitat hypothesis** of Binford and others essentially says that populations have a maximum carrying capacity or number of organisms that be supported in a given area. At the end of the Pleistocene epoch, the lushness of food resources increased population growth and sedentism in some areas. This eventually drove some people to move to marginal areas where competitive pressures compelled them toward domestication of plants and animals. The **sedentism and population growth hypothesis** of O. Henry suggests that the environmental shift caused certain groups to forsake foraging and develop a strategy for a more sedentary lifestyle. If this lifestyle was threatened, they tried to maintain it by altering their settlement patterns and attempting domestication.

Hypotheses About Origins of Agriculture Not Centered on Development of Sedentary Lifestyle

The co-**evolution hypothesis** of Rindos contends that human groups evolved along with changes in food sources in a symbiotic or mutually beneficial relationship. In other words, humans did not intentionally domesticate certain plants and animals but rather subsistence strategies just naturally evolved into practices that maximized output and the evolutionary fitness of man, plants, and animals. Braidwood, in his **readiness hypothesis**, theorizes that knowledge obtained by groups led to domestication and agriculture. Cultural and historical readiness, not lifestyle or environmental factors, prompted these advancements. Other hypotheses include the **dump heap**

hypothesis of Anderson, which states that certain plants prospered in areas that were disturbed by human use, and the **demographic hypothesis** of Boserup, which argues that population explosions lead to more rigorous subsistence tactics.

Contributions of Hydraulic Systems and Trade to Development of States

Some experts contend that the development of **irrigation** and later **hydraulic systems** to control water contributed greatly to development of states and civilizations. For example, Wittfogal proposed in his **hydraulic hypothesis** that the necessity to increase agricultural production logically leads to development and later control of water resources (such as canals and aqueducts). **Political structures** become necessary to regulate water production and mediate conflicts. There are documented examples, such as Mesopotamia and Egypt, in which there is a direct correlation between development of hydraulic systems and creation of states. Some believe that states appeared in crucial places along **long-distance trade routes**. This theory is debatable, because states sometimes formed before trade routes or trade was prevalent in regions that never developed states.

State, Empire, and Civilization

Traditionally, a **state** is a culture with a centralized authority, specialized administrative roles such as tax collection and law enforcement, and a stratified class system. The term **civilization** is fairly similar and may be used interchangeably, although it implies a certain level of complexity and refinement. A civilization is a culture in which there is an abundant food supply, labor specialization, an official governmental structure, social stratification, large building projects, and recordkeeping. An established state often develops into an **empire**, which encompasses a larger territory than a state, incorporates more and larger systems, and whose power is primarily based on military endeavors.

Carneiro's Theory of State Formation

According to Robert Carneiro, **states** are formed because of the confluence of three aspects. Implicit in **Caneiro's theory** is initial cultivation and food production. First, the **environmental resources** must be restricted either physically (by water boundaries for example) or socially (such as nearby societies). Next, the **population** has to be increased. Lastly, **fighting** develops and intensifies between factions. This multivariate type of theory provides a good explanation for development of some states such as those in coastal Peru, but does not have universal application. There are societies with three of these factors that did not develop into states.

Features Distinguishing Early States or Civilizations from Prior Societal Forms

Early states or civilizations differed from prior societal forms in that they:

- Were controlled by a formal government extending over a specific region. Power was generally gained through expansionism and conquest.
- Had highly productive farming economies and a food and labor excess. Usually also had some form of irrigation or water control.
- Had densely populated communities.
- Were stratified into fixed social classes controlled by an elite group through coercion.
- Had specialized labor divisions and artisans. Used some form of taxation to support the specialists.

- Constructed monumental public buildings, other architecture such as temples and pyramids, and great engineering works.
- Formulated some type of recordkeeping system such as a written script or hieroglyphics.

Tribe, Chiefdom, and State

A tribe is a society in which there is no formal, powerful ruler. A **tribe** is based primarily on kinship. Tribes often have some individuals with increased prestige and some leadership authority but no absolute power. A **chiefdom** is a slightly more complex political structure in which chiefs have more authority in certain areas, but this clout is not absolute or exclusive. Chiefdoms are usually centered on religious beliefs, and they have no formal governmental structure. Early **states**, described in more detail elsewhere, were controlled by an elite class with considerably more authority obtained through coercion.

Earliest Towns or Chiefdoms in Southwestern Asia

Jericho, now a modern city in Israel, and **Catal Huyuk** (or Catalhoyuk), in the central region of current-day Turkey, were two of the earliest known **towns** in southwestern Asia. Jericho was a town at least 9000 years ago as evidenced by remains of a great wall built around it. Catalhoyuk arose about 9000 years ago as well and flourished from about 8000 to 7000 years ago. It was much larger than Jericho with a maze of interconnected mud-brick rooms that could be accessed through openings in the roof. Although the site is complex, the society was apparently decentralized and not socially stratified.

Egalitarian, Ranked Societies, and Stratified Societies

Egalitarian societies based on equality, such as bands or tribes, do not have inherited status differences. Instead, any eminence gained is based on age, gender, aptitudes, or achievement. Foragers were **egalitarian**. **Ranked societies**, such as chiefdoms and certain tribes, do have status differences, but these are based primarily on the hereditary distance from the chief and there is no social stratification. Some experts distinguish a ranked society that extended to more than one settlement and established hierarchy between settlements as a chiefdom. Some tribes, particularly Native Americans in the Pacific Northwest, had a ranked society but differ in that villages were separate and not ranked relative to another. A **stratified society** is one in which status differences were heritable and separated into distinct aristocratic and commoner classes. Stratified societies are known as states and associated (at least initially) with an agricultural based economy.

Earliest Known Chiefdoms in the Middle East

The earliest known **chiefdoms** in the Middle East were in the region known as **Mesopotamia**, geographically located between the Tigris and Euphrates rivers. Between approximately 7500 and 6000 years ago, the Halafian and Ubaid cultures thrived in northern and southern Mesopotamia (both regions of present-day Iraq). The **Halafian culture** produced a characteristic graceful pottery style. These cultures are considered chiefdoms because they utilized striking trinkets as markers of different degrees of status which were buried with the dead. There are also indications that the Halafian villages may have had some form of alliance. Another chiefdom was **Tell Hamoukar** in northeastern Syria.

Uruk Period in the Middle East

The Uruk period in southern Mesopotamia followed the Ubaid period starting about 6000 years ago. The period is named after the city located there named **Ur**. Ur is known for its great **ziggurat**

- 112 -

(dated ~4100 years before the present), a monumental mud-brick temple tower shaped like a rectangular platform with stairs to the top. Cities had emerged by this time and there were central forms of government. This period and area also produced the earliest forms of writing, believed to be invented 5600 years ago. The people used *cuneiform writing* in which wedge-shaped impressions were cut into clay. *Metallurgy*, the mining and processing of metals to create tools, was perfected about 5000 years ago in bronze (from copper alloys), gold, and iron. **Sumer**, a city in the southern portion, produced a culture with cites enclosed by fortress walls. By 4600 years ago, the ruling class structures were secular in nature and societies were stratified.

Four Great Early River Valley States in the Old World

The following are four great early river valley states in the Old World:

- **In ancient Mesopotamia and Babylonia** - This area, discussed more fully on other cards, is considered by many to be the cradle of civilization. It is located between the Tigris and Euphrates rivers.
- **Along the Nile River in ancient Egypt** - Civilization started in northern Africa. Iron smelting was perfected and spread. The major linguistic family in the region, Bantu, was spread to many other areas in Africa through migration. This led to the Mwenemutapa empire in gold-rich Zimbabwe and the fortressed state of Great Zimbabwe about 700 years ago.
- **Along the Indus River Valley** - The first evidence was the Harappan state from about 4600 years ago in modern-day Pakistan, which thrived until 3900 years ago. Many other cities and smaller towns existed along the valley and along the Ganges River into India.
- **Along the Yellow River** - Located in northern China, the earliest state here was the Shang dynasty starting around 3800 years ago.

Development of Civilization in Egypt

Civilization developed in ancient Egypt along the **Nile River**, which provided opportunities for agriculture. Initially, certain towns that were strategically positioned for trade grew into central places or small city-states with rulers. Around 5500 years ago, the most significant centers were Hierakonpolis, Abydos, and Nagada. Excavations of Hierakonpolis indicate that there was mud-based housing for at least 2500 people, elaborate burials indicating an elite class, and a thriving pottery business. Within a few hundred years, expansion attempts and warfare among different city-states led to the **unification of Egypt**. **Narmer** (also called Menes) from Hierakonpolis was the first ruler of this unified Egypt around 5100 years ago. Some of the crowning achievements in ancient Egypt are the pyramids, including the first built by King Djoser about 4700 years ago in Saqqara, and the later three great pyramids at Giza.

Development of Civilization in the Indus Valley

The oldest known Neolithic sites along the Indus Valley were in **Baluchistan** in western Pakistan, including Mehrgarh from about 7100 years ago. Inhabitants from Mehrgarh engaged in agriculture, domestication of cattle, and apparently traded with distant areas. By 5000 years ago, the **Nal culture** developed in the region and built dams to control flooding. This technology enabled further population growth near the Indus River until about 4500 years ago; at least five large urban areas developed, surrounded by farmlands that helped supported each. The sites of **Mohenjo-Daro** and **Harappa** (perhaps the first real state in the area, about 4600 years ago) are prime examples. The center of each was the citadel or fortress, the homes had private bathrooms connected to a sewer system, there were specialized artisans, the streets were carefully laid in a grid pattern, and there was a symbol-based recordkeeping system.

Development of Civilization in China

The first civilization in China, the **Shang civilization** or dynasty, developed from the Neolithic Lung-shan culture. The **Lung-shan people** were the first completely agricultural group in the region starting about 6000 years ago. They and their descendants also domesticated animals and hunted. The first known site that could be classified a civilization was at **Erh-li-t'ou** on the Lo River in the Honan province in northeastern China from about 3800 years ago. The site contains bronze and jade artifacts, two palaces, and evidence of social stratification in the form of differences in burial practices. Another settlement near **Cheng-chou** was even larger and had many elements indicative of social stratification; the site is surrounded by a great wall with other living and industrials arrangements outside the wall.

Early Olmec Chiefdoms in Mesoamerica

Mesoamerica extends from southern North America into Central America. Several early chiefdoms and states came from this region, particularly from areas in Mexico and Guatemala. There are three known **Olmec sites** along the southern Gulf Coast region of Mexico, established 3200 to 2500 years ago. They appear to have been early chiefdoms and are known for their enormous carved stone heads. The Olmecs engaged in commerce with other groups in **Mesoamerica**, particularly those from the western Oaxaca Valley in Mexico. There were about twenty-five self-governing chiefdoms in the region at this time. The shift toward development of states was probably facilitated in part by the interchanging of ideas between the various chiefdoms.

Formation of the Zapotec State

The Zapotec state, located in the western Mexican Oaxaca Valley, was the earliest Mesoamerican state. **Monte Alban** was the capital of a chiefdom from approximately 500 B.C. until about 100 A.D. (A.D.) when it shifted toward being a state and continued until it dispersed into smaller principalities around 700 A.D. There is considerable evidence that the Zapotec state formation occurred through invasion of other distant political units to the north, west, and southwest. Buildings found at Monte Alban indicate a highly specialized bureaucracy and include large stone hieroglyphics describing conquests. There were also palaces and temples.

Early States in the Valley of Mexico

The Valley of Mexico is in central Mexico near present-day Mexico City. It is basically a valley bounded by mountains. Inhabitants primarily occupied the more temperate, wetter regions in the southern section of the valley until about 2500 years ago. At that time, novel maize varieties were developed and some irrigation was being done, allowing for population increase and expansion north. The town of **Teotihuacan** thrived in the valley starting around 1900 years ago, developing into the first state in the Valley of Mexico by 100 A.D. (A.D.). It continued to flourish until 700 A.D. (when the population became more scattered) and became the earliest Mesoamerican empire. Teotihuacan was a planned city based on a grid pattern centered on the imposing **Pyramid of the Sun**. It had a settlement hierarchy indicating a state structure, great irrigation systems and other architecture were built, there was specialization in roles, and there was status stratification. The major city emerging later during the Aztec period (~1325 to 1520 A.D.) was **Tenochtitlan**, where Mexico City is now located. This emergence was primarily due to increased agricultural and trade activities.

- 114 -

Mayan Civilization

The Maya were one of the regional civilizations that developed in Mesoamerica after the Olmec. A number of cities developed starting approximately 2300 years ago in the areas of modern Honduras, Belize, Guatemala, and the lowlands of Mexico. Most of the early Mayan **public architecture** is related to their religion and the religious elite, such as the temple at **Dzibilchaltun**. Their main agricultural product was **maize**. The Mayans were a full-fledged civilization by about 1900 years ago, reaching their peak about 250 A.D. (the Classical period). The Mayans had a royal elite class, social stratification, monumental constructions, artwork, a written language in the form of hieroglyphics, a numbering system, and two types of calendars. During the Classical period, there were as many as fifty politically autonomous urban areas. The vast majority of Mayans were farmers and their agricultural techniques probably contributed to their decline. They used relatively unproductive slash-and-burn methods which depleted the soil of nutrients, causing erosion and deforestation.

Origins and Evolution of Civilization in South America

As early as 5200 years ago, there were a number of populated sites in river valleys north of current day Lima, Peru. Each had stone edifices including flat-topped pyramids and large plazas. The site at **Caral** along the Supe River, which dates to approximately 4500 years ago, had six pyramids, which apparently housed the elite. The residents subsisted on a variety of domesticated plants (such as squash, beans, and sweet potato) and shellfish. Over the years, the various communities became isolated from one another. However, by 3000 years ago, the **Chavin religious artistic style** was prevalent throughout the region and served to unite the different valley cultures. This style depicts animals and humans with jaguar features in sculpture, often using the decorating method called **repousse** in which gold or other metals are hammered from the reverse side. The **Moche culture** developed on the northern coast of Peru around 1900 years ago and is characterized by distinctive naturalistic pottery; a well-known site is the Pyramid of the Sun. Subsequent states in the region were the Tiwanaku and Huari around 1400 to 1200 years ago and the Chimu, which emerged about 1000 years ago.

Inca Empire

The Inca Empire or **Tawantinsuyu** reigned between 1476 and 1534 A.D. from northern Ecuador to southern Chile. The ethnic Inca were a small minority of the population in the empire but they expanded and ruled through military or other types of coercion. The Inca set up administrative operations in each conquered state with an ethnic Incan as governor and concentrated operations in **Cuzco**. The Inca imposed their language, **Quechua** (which continues today), on all those they conquered. They did not impose their religion, however, and embraced local gods into their beliefs. The Incas are known for their estate at **Machu Picchu** in the Andes, especially the manner in which walls were constructed by the precise fitting of stones instead of any type of bonding material. They were also fine metallurgists.

Early Civilizations in Southern Europe

The first European civilization was the **Minoan culture of Crete**, which started about 4000 years ago. The capital was **Knossos**, Crete, where there are still remnants of an extensive **Labyrinth** or palace. The Minoan culture was central to olive and other trade in the Aegean portion of the Mediterranean. Another civilization called the **Mycenaean** began to dominate around 3400 years ago on mainland Greece. The Mycenaeans primarily traded copper and tin. Their supremacy was short-lived, only a few hundred years, before other Greek states emerged as predominant.

Early African Civilizations Outside of Egypt

Nubia, the region of the Nile Valley just south of Egypt into Sudan, produced several civilizations dating back as far as 3500 years ago. A famous site associated with the ancient Nubians is at **Meroe**, dated somewhere near 2000 years ago, which consists of many mud brick monumental structures. There is another ancient city to the southeast of Nubia called **Axum** in contemporary Ethiopia characterized by very tall stone towers. A walled city called **Jenne-jeno** existed in Mali more than 1000 years ago. By about 700 years ago, the **Great Zimbabwe** of southern Africa was built as the capital of an extensive political entity.

Significant Ancient Civilizations in North America and Southeast Asia

In North America, the most significant ancient civilization was at **Cahokia** along the Mississippi River near East St. Louis, Illinois. Cahokia was the hub of a Native American chiefdom for at least 500 years starting around a thousand years ago. The site is called **Cahokia Mounds** because it is characterized by a series of mounds (included the enormous Monk's Mound) surrounded by a log wall. There is evidence of social stratification and labor specialization. Other earlier North American cultures include the **Hopewell** and the **Adena**. In the area of modern Cambodia, the **Khmer civilization** thrived from approximately 800 to 1300 A.D. They built a series of grand temples during this period, the largest and most elaborate being at **Angkor Wat**, and a string of gigantic reservoirs and canals

Molecular Anthropology

Molecular anthropology is a subdivision of physical anthropology that utilizes genetic analysis of DNA to determine evolutionary linkage. **DNA**, or deoxyribonucleic acid, is the substance that carries the genetic information of humans (and other organisms). DNA can be taken from fossils, for example, and compared to other ancient artifacts or the blood of living humans or other primates. Typically, molecular anthropologists look at relationships between antique and modern species, patterns of migration, or patterns of divergence. Much of this is accomplished by examining **haplogroups** or clusters of hereditary traits indicative of geographical origin.

Precedents for the Theory of Evolution

Charles Darwin's theory of evolution (discussed further elsewhere) was preceded by work and concepts of other researchers. In the 1700s, **Carolus Linnaeus** put together an extensive taxonomic classification of plants and animals, which was based on similarities and differences in physical attributes. Although he believed in creationism or divine creation of all things in the universe, Linnaeus' scheme provided a useful basis for later work and is still significant. Around the same time and into the 19th century, fossil records were being gathered that were counterintuitive to creationism as they showed discrepancies between these records and existing plants and animals. Darwin's father, **Erasmus**, was an evolutionist, writing a book called *Zoonomia* in 1794 in which he supported the shared ancestry of all animal species. Charles Darwin was also persuaded by the geologist **Sir Charles Lyell**, who put forth the concept of **uniformitarianism**, which said that natural forces operating then also explained past events and disputed the creationist theories of the age of earth.

Charles Darwin's Theory of Evolution

Charles Darwin set forth a theory of evolution or development from earlier forms or species. He coauthored a paper with Alfred Russel Wallace, who had similar views, in 1858 and published *On the Origin of the Species* in 1859. Much of Darwin's work was predicated by studying finches in the

Galapagos. His theory is based on the process of **natural selection** or the preferential choosing of forms that have features that facilitate reproductive success. Organisms within a group vary, and those with characteristics that help them thrive and reproduce are more likely to pass on their characteristics. That is, they have an adaptive advantage. Evolution and natural selection illustrate the effect of environment on the genetic material that is more likely to be passed on to future generations, but they do not suggest that acquired characteristics are passed on.

Mendelian Genetics

Mendelian genetics is based on experiments performed by interbreeding of pea plants by **Gregor Mendel** in the 1850s. When Mendel crossed pure strains of pea plants with different characteristics, all F_1 or first generation plants had similar **phenotypes** or outward physical characteristics. However, when he did further breeding between different F_1 plants, the F_2 or second generation plants exhibited more than one phenotype. These observations led Mendel to postulate that there was a **dominant** form or trait that could conceal a **recessive** trait that was still present and could be passed on. The actual genetic makeup of an organism is its genotype, which we now know to be carried on chromosomes containing paired DNA (deoxyribonucleic acid) and made up of genes or basic hereditary units for various traits. **Alleles** are possible variants of genes. If an organism has identical alleles, they are said to be **homozygous**, whereas if they have inherited two alleles that are slightly different, they are said to be **heterozygous** and will express the dominant allele.

Mendel's Views on Independent Assortment and Recombination

Gregor Mendel did additional work beyond that for which he originally postulated Mendelian genetics. He developed a **law of independent assortment** based on his observations that different traits were inherited separately from others. For example, inheritance of seed shape, coat color, type of pod, or stem length differences could show up independently during interbreeding and recombine in many ways. This **recombination** generates varieties that can provide the basis for natural selection. However, Mendelian genetics and his laws on independent assortment and recombination only provide a static situation and do not address evolution and change through genetic mutation.

DNA

DNA or **deoxyribonucleic acid** is the fundamental hereditary material of life and the basis of biochemical or molecular genetics. Structurally in humans and many other organisms, DNA is a double-stranded helix. Each DNA strand is made up of many molecules of the sugar **deoxyribose**, which is chemically bound to one of four bases, either **thymine** (T), **adenine** (A), **cytosine** (C) or **guanine** (G). One DNA strand is bound to the other in the helix through A-T or C-G interactions. DNA can duplicate itself by unwinding the strands and forming new complementary ones, making it crucial to the production of gametes (cells involved with sexual reproduction) and new cells. It is also used to encode for the manufacturing of proteins by serving as a template for **RNA** (ribonucleic acid). Three RNA molecules in sequence, a triplet, code for a particular amino acid used to produce proteins like enzymes, hormones and antibodies. Changes that occur in DNA molecules are known as **mutations**, which account for the majority of shifts through natural selection.

Cell Division

Usually cell division occurs through a process called **mitosis**, in which a cell divides into two daughter chromosomes with the same number of chromosomes as the parent cell. Mitosis occurs through life and mistakes such as different types of mutations can cause diseases such as

- 117 -

malignancy. Sex cells or gametes undergo a slightly different course called **meiosis** in which a cell's nucleus divides into 4 nuclei each containing half the usual number of chromosomes. Each allele pair is broken up (called segregation by Mendel). When a male gamete or sperm fertilizes the female egg or ovum, a **zygote** is formed which grows rapidly into a child. Most cells have 23 pairs of chromosomes whereas a gamete has 23 individual ones. Fertilization can result in a variety of combinations accounting for the range in characteristics in progeny. Diversity can also result from an early event during meiosis called **crossing over**, which is the intertwining and subsequent swapping of some DNA on homologous chromosomes in gametes.

Genetic Mutations

Mutations in sex cells are hereditary; those in other somatic cells can cause disease. A **base substitution** or **single point mutation** is the substitution of one single base for another. If the mutation changes the amino acid that is encoded for, abnormal proteins associated with a disease state may be produced. **Chromosomal rearrangement** is a mutation in which part of a chromosome breaks and pieces are rearranged and reattached in a different configuration. It can transpire in a gamete, in the fertilized egg, or in other growing cells. Chromosomal rearrangement is primarily responsible for speciation, hereditary disorders, and malignancies.

Gene Pools and Genetic Evolution

The term gene pool is a collective expression for the entirety of genetic material in a breeding population or **deme**. A **gene pool** includes all alleles, genes, chromosomes and genotypes in that population. **Genetic evolution** refers to the shift in gene (in other words allele) frequency in a breeding population from one generation to the next. Most evolution results from the genetic transmission of variety through mutations which facilitate selective advantages. Other underlying forces that can play a role in genetic evolution include natural selection, random genetic drift, and gene flow.

Natural Selection

According to natural selection, individuals with **phenotypes** that thrive in a particular environment are selected over those with less favorable phenotypes or evident characteristics. Phenotypes can mask true genotype or genetic makeup if the organism possesses heterozygous alleles. Nevertheless, over time the features that are most adaptive or favored by natural selection will be preferentially selected. This means that there will be **directional selection** and eventual removal from the gene pool of recessive alleles that do not adapt well. Environmental changes can alter the directional selection and favor other phenotypes for certain traits. **Sexual selection** is a form of natural selection where organisms prefer to mate with a member of the opposite sex with a particular characteristic, such as feather color for birds or body shape for humans. There can also be a **balanced polymorphism**, in which two or more alleles for a trait tend to be passed on at relatively constant rate because each has equivalent advantages and disadvantages in a particular environment.

Random Genetic Drift

Random genetic drift is genetic change over generations that occurs coincidentally. Certain traits are passed on in a nonrandom fashion and eventually genotypic ratios change or traits are lost. The complete displacement of one trait over another is referred to as **fixation**, which can transpire more quickly in small populations. One type of **genetic drift** is **fission** in which a population splits for some reason to form new subpopulations. If there is an uneven split, a **founder effect** is said to occur. Genetic drift can also occur through **gamete sampling**. As genes are passed from one

- 118 -

generation to the next, a large number of genetic combinations are possible during fertilization, which are unrelated to adaptation. Over generations, significant genetic drift can be observed in a population.

Random Gene Flow

Gene flow is the swapping of genetic material through breeding with other groups. Traditionally, populations in relatively close proximity often **interbreed**, and genes are passed along. The sequence of interbreeding can continue to other groups as well. At some point, gene flow may contribute to **natural selection** depending on the environment. Generally, gene flow can only occur within a species, which is a group of organisms that are genetically similar enough to create offspring that can survive and reproduce. Thus, gene flow can usually produce variety but not speciation or the development of new species.

Modern Synthesis Viewpoint on Evolution

The modern synthesis viewpoint on evolution integrates Darwin's theory of evolution with Mendelian genetics. It holds that new species can only occur when they are reproductively inaccessible to another. Genetic changes that transpire without resultant speciation are examples of **microevolution**. More momentous changes that occur over longer periods of time can produce speciation and are considered **macroevolution**. **Speciation** is the separation of a particular ancestral species into one or several successors. Both micro- and macroevolution occur via similar mechanisms such as mutations. The rate at which microevolutionary changes eventually lead to macroevolution is not usually consistent, as Darwin originally postulated. Contemporary models are built on the idea of **punctuated equilibrium**, or lengthy periods of stability interspersed with occasional evolutionary jumps. There are many possible explanations for punctuated equilibrium, such as extinction followed by invasion, substitution of a group with a highly adaptive trait, and the acceleration of certain transformations due to abrupt environmental changes.

Racial Classification for Human Diversity

Racial classification categorizes organisms supposedly based on some sort of common ancestry. **Phenotypical traits** believed to show shared genetic ancestry are selected as the basis of racial classification. For humans, early racial classification schemes were based on skin color. Today, an explanatory methodology concentrating on the understanding of certain differences is favored over racial classification schemes. This is because the so-called "races" are not biologically different. Traditional classifications identified three races as white, black, and yellow or Caucasoid, Negroid, and Mongoloid. However, skin colors vary widely, certain populations are not easily classified by these schemes, various combinations of features that might be considered important can occur, and phenotype is not always reflective of underlying genotype.

American Anthropological Association's *Statement on "Race"*

In 1998, the American Anthropological Association (AAA) issued a *Statement on "Race."* The statement says that there is more **variation** within so-called "racial" groups than between, and that historically all interacting groups have tended to **interbreed**. It further states that most diversity has occurred gradually and since physical traits are passed on independently of one another, racial classifications are **arbitrary** and **biased**. In addition, the AAA Statement declared that previously the notion of race was used mostly to impose and reinforce status differences. Eventually, the concept of "race" developed into a world view. It is the view of the AAA that all normal individuals have the ability to learn any cultural behavior and that any contemporary differences in performance between certain "racial" groups are the result of factors other than biological inheritance.

Factors That Determine Skin Color

There are many genes that affect **skin color**, although the exact number is unknown. Skin color is mainly determined by the relative amount of the chemical **melanin** in a person's epidermis or surface layer of skin. People with darker skins have more melanin, a natural sunscreen. Before the sixteenth century, most extremely dark-skinned persons occupied the tropics, a zone 23 degrees to either side of the equator. People living outside this tropical zone had lighter skin colors that gradually got lighter the further they were from the tropic zone. However, newer migratory patterns such as Asians moving to eventually produce Native Americans caused different skin color patterns. Historically, geographic differences in skin color were a result of natural selection, whereas later migration and today's technological advances lessened its significance in terms of skin color.

Advantages and Disadvantages of Dark Versus Light Skin Colors

People with a dark skin color have high levels of skin **melanin** which naturally screens out UV radiation, averts sunburn and consequently increases sweating as well as thermoregulation. **Thermoregulation** is the maintenance of a steady body temperature despite environmental changes. Individuals with dark skin color are less susceptible to diseases, skin cancer, and folate breakdown. **Folate** is an essential nutrient used in cell division and DNA assembly. Disadvantages of dark skin color are a reduced ultraviolet radiation absorption outside tropical areas which makes them more prone to bone diseases like rickets and osteoporosis because they cannot produce vitamin D from sunlight exposure. People with light skin color have no natural sunscreen, but the UV exposure does permit the body to produce vitamin D and lessen the possibility of rickets or osteoporosis. The negatives of light skin color are increased susceptibility to sunburn, disease, skin cancer, and folate destruction (leading possibly to neural tube defects in the fetus and diseases like spina bifida). Light skin color can impair spermatogenesis, depress sweating, and decrease thermoregulation.

Relationships Between Blood Groups, Adaptation, and Variation

The basis of blood grouping is the **ABO system**, which distinguishes people's red blood cells in terms of their **surface antigens**. There are 3 possible **alleles** (A, B or O), and combinations of these alleles give four possible **phenotypes** (A, B, AB, or O). A and B antigens trigger antibody production. These antigens are made up of protein and sugars. It has been demonstrated that individuals with certain ABO blood types are more susceptible to certain diseases. In particular, before smallpox was essentially eradicated in the 1970s, it was found that people with types A or AB blood were more prone to the disease, probably because the virus is antigenically similar to the A antigen. Therefore, A or AB individuals do not recognize it as foreign and do not make protective antibodies. The most prevalent group worldwide, type O individuals with neither an A nor B surface antigen, are apparently more prone to cholera, bubonic plague, and gastric ulcers.

Relationships Between Hemoglobin Subtypes and Disease

Hemoglobin is an iron-containing protein present in the red blood cells (RBCs) that transports oxygen. The normal **hemoglobin** allele is Hb^A, but there is another possible allele, Hb^S. People who are **homozygous** for the Hb^S allele have sickle-cell anemia characterized by crescent-shaped RBCs, inability to store oxygen, clogging of small blood vessels, and increased incidence of fatality. On the other hand, individuals who are **heterozygous**, Hb^A/Hb^S or sickle-cell trait, appear to be less

- 120 -

susceptible to malaria because malarial parasites cannot flourish in the abnormal hemoglobin yet the normal component wards off sickle-cell anemia. In areas where malaria is prevalent, the Hb^S is protective, making it in effect a genetic anti-malarial "drug." Other adaptations related to hemoglobin have been observed, such as Andeans who have developed the capacity to produce more hemoglobin and store more oxygen in response to the thin air in the region.

Influence of Natural Selection and Adaptation on Facial Features

Several facial features have been correlated with environmental differences. In particular, nose length has been statistically shown to follow **Thomson's nose rule**, which says that the average nose length increases in cold regions. This is an adaptive response because in a longer nose there are more membranes and blood vessels to moisten and warm the air as it is inhaled, making it advantageous in both dry and cold areas. Large average **tooth size** has been associated with populations such as Native Australians who traditionally were hunters and gatherers.

Influence of Natural Selection and Adaptation on Size and Body Build

Different body sizes have adaptive advantages in different climates. There is a tenet called **Bergmann's rule** which states that for two bodies of similar shape, the smaller one has more surface area per unit of weight and loses heat more. Therefore, **larger body sizes** which retain heat more effectively are more likely to be found in colder areas, and **smaller body sizes** are more prevalent in hotter regions. Observations on body shape tend to support **Allen's rule**, which asserts that body parts that stick out, such as limbs, digits, and ears, tend to be longer or larger in groups from warmer climates. The rationale is that this increases the surface area comparative to mass and allows for heat loss.

Reading of the Genetic Code of an Individual Cell

Cells consist of a **nucleus** containing chromosomes and the cytoplasm containing other structures serving other functions. **Chromosomes** are made up of a protein core with two strands of deoxyribonucleic acid (DNA) wrapped around them in a double helical formation bound through interactions between complementary bases, either A-T (adenine-thymine) or G-C (guanine-cytosine). During **replication**, the helix uncoils and the now unpaired bases pick up their complementary bases in solution. Thus when the cell divides during **mitosis**, there are two daughter cells with the same number of chromosomes. Partial unwinding of the helix allows for synthesis of proteins. Here, part of one strand of the DNA is used as a template for transcription by **messenger ribonucleic acid** (mRNA) which uses complementary bases, except that uracil (U) is substituted for thymine. The mRNA leaves the nucleus and travels to the ribosomes in the cytoplasm where transfer RNA (tRNA) reads the codes for production of amino acids and assembly of proteins. Each section of three nucleotides in DNA is a codon for a particular **amino acid**.

Human Genome

An organism's total genetic constitution is its **genome**. There was a **Human Genome Project** completed in 2003 that sequenced almost the complete human genome. Two different groups sequenced the genome of two different individuals. While work and analysis continues, 3.1 million base pairs were sequenced. It was found that the vast majority (as much as 98%) of DNA is **non-coding**, meaning it does not code for proteins. Functions of non-coding DNA include initiation and termination of coding sequences, regulation of gene function, and transport of other DNA. Coding sections are interspersed with non-coding ones. A **coding sequence** can code for multiple proteins depending on which portion is transcribed. There are RNAs with functions other than ciphering the

- 121 -

protein code, mostly as regulatory agents. It also appears that some DNA coding sequences are designed to produce these non-coding RNAs instead of proteins.

Equations Relevant to Genetics of Populations

For a particular allele assuming two forms (A and B):

- Calculate the **allele count**
  - Number of A alleles = (2 x no. of homozygous AA individuals) + no. of heterozygous individuals (AB)
  - Number of B alleles = (2 x no. of homozygous BB individuals) + no. of heterozygous individuals (AB)
  - Total allele count = no. of A alleles + no. of B alleles
- Calculate **frequency** of each allele
  - Frequency of A allele = no. of A alleles/total allele count = p
  - Frequency of B allele = no. B alleles/total allele count = q

Then the **Hardy-Weinberg equilibrium hypothesis**, which assumes the null hypothesis of no evolutionary change, is used to test the impact of evolution. From above, all genotypes should be the sum of the product of frequencies, thus in theory $p^2 + 2pq + q^2 = 1$. The null hypothesis can be tested by:

- Calculate expected frequency for each genotype by using p and q from above.
- Multiply each expected frequency by total number of individuals in population to get expected number for each.
- Compare expected and observed numbers for each genotype. If they do not concur, the null hypothesis is refuted.

Taxonomy of Primates

Taxonomy is a classification scheme for organisms that assigns them to certain categories or taxa based on their relationships and likenesses to other organisms. Many resemblances reflect their shared **phylogeny** or genetic relatedness. Organisms in the same category have **homologies** or traits that were inherited from the same ancestor. The levels of **zoological taxonomy** start with a kingdom at the top and go down through phylum, subphylum, class, infraclass, order, suborder, infraorder, super family, family, tribe, genus, species, and finally subspecies. Humans and other primates fit into the kingdom of Animalia or animals. The category of primates is at the order level, and it includes monkeys and apes in addition to humans. In fact, the field of primatology studies nonhuman primates including ancient and living apes, monkeys, and prosimians.

Human's Place in the Scheme of Primates

The term **primate** describes a member of a mammalian order with a large brain and complex hands and feet. There are two suborders, Prosimii or prosimians, and Anthropoidea or anthropoids. Prosimians are lower order nocturnal primates such as lemurs fitting into three infraorders and so on. Anthropoids are divided into two infraorders. One infraorder is Platyrrhini or platyrrhines with wide nostrils, notably New World monkeys. The other is Catarrhini or catarrhines, which includes Old World monkeys, apes, and humans. Categorically below that, catarrhines are separated into two super families of Cercopithecoidea, which includes Old World monkeys, and Hominoidea or hominids comprised of three families. These families are Hylobatidae with gibbons and siamangs, Pongidae represented by orangutans, and Hominidae or hominids, to which gorillas, chimpanzees, and humans all belong. Modern humans are of the family Hominidae (hominids), tribe Hominini or hominins, genus Homo or human, species Homo sapiens (which also includes recent humans), and subspecies Homo sapiens sapiens.

Relationship Between Homologies, Analogies, and Convergent Evolution

The term **homology** refers to traits actually inherited from a common ancestor. **Analogies** are resemblances that have arisen through convergent evolution. In **convergent evolution**, analogous selective forces have acted on different organisms to generate similar adaptive traits. Thus, it appears that the two are closely related because of similar traits, but in fact they are not. Ideal taxonomic classifications rely only on homology, not analogy. Humans definitely fit into the same zoological family of hominid as previous humans, chimpanzees, gorillas, and other common predecessors.

Primate Tendencies of Anthropoids

Anthropoids are the suborder of the order primates to which humans as well as monkeys and apes belong. Early primates were arboreal tree dwellers, and thus all contemporary primates have characteristics reflecting this. Primates are distinguished by **five basic traits**. The first is the ability to grasp by having flexible five-digited hands and feet. Humans and some other primates also have opposable thumbs that can contact other fingers. Humans have lost this trait for their feet as they have adapted to upright, bipedal walking. Primates have a better sense of sight than smell. The primary tactile or touch organ in primates is the hand, mainly the fingerprint area. Primates have larger brains relative to body size and more brain matter devoted to cognition than other mammals. Most primates also have only one offspring, increasing prospects for developing learned conduct. Lastly, primates are generally very social.

Prosimians

Prosimians are the other suborder of primates besides anthropoids. Lemurs, lorises, and tarsiers fit into the Prosimii or prosimian suborder. The **prosimians** that have survived to the present day have done so primarily because they were active nocturnally and did not have to vie for survival with anthropoids that operated diurnally or mainly during the day. Today, the native habitat of prosimians is Madagascar for lemurs; Indonesia, Malaysia, and the Philippines for the tarsier; and Africa and Asia for lorises. Fossils show, however, that prosimians once lived in North American and Europe.

New World and Old World Monkeys

New World and Old World monkeys were reproductively inaccessible to the other. Both are anthropoids, but **New World monkeys** belong to the infraorder of platyrrhines characterized by a flat nose and often a prehensile or grasping tail. They are found in Central and South American forests. **Old World monkeys** belong to the infraorder of catarrhines which also includes apes and humans. All catarrhines have more pointed or sharp noses. Larger Old World monkeys like baboons and some macaques are generally terrestrial, whereas smaller examples tend to be arboreal and live in trees. The terrestrial species often show sexual dimorphism or trait differences between the sexes. All monkeys have arms and legs that are approximately of equal length, distinguishing them from apes and humans.

Characteristics of Apes

Apes and humans form the superfamily of **hominoids**, separate from the superfamily of Cercopithecoidea (Old World monkeys). Apes include the larger orangutans, gorillas, chimpanzees, and technically humans as well as the smaller gibbons and siamangs. The largest distinction between apes and other anthropoids is that they have **arms** that are longer than their legs. This enables them to swing under and across branches through trees using their hands, an ability called **brachiation**. Adults and larger apes that cannot brachiate safely due to weight have now adapted to terrestrial movement. Nevertheless, the way in which the shoulder and collarbone of both apes and humans are constructed indicates that all had a common brachiating predecessor.

Smaller Apes

The smaller apes include gibbons and siamangs, which are sometimes known as the "lesser apes." Both usually reside in **primary groups** with a bonded male, female, and preadolescent progeny. Gibbons are mainly arboreal and have lengthy arms and fingers facilitating brachiation as well as balance on the occasions they walk upright. They are very slim and nimble compared to other larger apes. A typical gibbon is only about a meter tall and weighs only 5 to 10 kilograms (up to 25 pounds). Their natural habitat is the forests of Southeast Asia. They eat fruits and sometimes insects or small animals.

Orangutans

Orangutans are considered "great apes" along with gorillas and chimpanzees. There are two extant species in the jungles of Asia that are part of the genus **Pongo** and the only representatives of the family Pongidae. Orangutans exhibit a high degree of sexual dimorphism, with the adult male much heavier than the female. The mature males are smaller than gorillas but larger than chimpanzees. Females and children are primarily arboreal whereas heavier males usually climb trees. They eat fruits, bark, leaves, and insects. Males tend to go out alone searching for food leaving the female and youngsters.

Gorillas

Gorillas are the most massive of apes. There are three extant subspecies of the species, which is technically called *Gorilla gorilla.* The native habitat of the smallest is various areas of Africa, the slightly bigger eastern lowland gorilla is found only in the Congo, and the biggest and rarest mountain gorillas are scattered. Just like orangutans, gorillas exhibit sexual dimorphism, with the male about twice as large as the adult female. Gorillas are for the most part terrestrial primates because although they have long arms reflecting their ancestry, they are too heavy to swing from trees. They eat a variety of primarily ground level vegetation. They are very social and tend to live in groups of up to 30 gorillas with one mature silverback gorilla as the lone breeding male.

Chimpanzees

Chimpanzees are the smallest of the so-called "great apes." There are two extant species, *Pan troglodytes* and *Pan paniscus,* which belong to the hominid family, genus **Pan**. A *Pan troglodyte* is the common chimpanzee, whose native habitat is various areas of Africa. They live primarily in tropical rain forests but are also found in woodlands or mixed regions. They eat mainly fruits but also small animals, eggs, and insects. The average adult female to male height is comparable to that in humans or .88 to 1. They are primarily arboreal, very social, and form a variety of social groups. The other representative species is *Pan paniscus,* the bonobo or pygmy chimpanzee. Bonobos are found only in the Democratic Republic of Congo in moist forests, and they have always been

- 124 -

arboreal. They are similar in size and female to male ratio as other chimpanzees. Their groupings are female-centric, and they have unusually frequent but often aggressive sex.

Behavioral Ecology and Fitness as Related to Primates

Behavioral ecology is the analysis of the evolutionary basis for social behaviors. It presumes the impact of natural selection, differential reproduction, and reproductive fitness. The concept of **fitness** means the ability to produce offspring that survive and reproduce. However, different social organizations in various primates illustrate diverse types of fitness. Some, like gibbons with strong male-female pair bonds, emphasize **individual fitness**, which is fitness quantified by the number of one's direct descendants. Others underscore **inclusive fitness**, the number of genes shared with relatives, evident in primates who defend the offspring of siblings.

Geological Time Scales

Geological times scales divide life as far back as that identified through fossil records. There are six eras and periods and epochs within all except the earliest eras. Fossils found in the same **stratum** or layer of earth are from the same time period or era. The oldest **Hadean era** began 4500 million years ago, the second oldest **Archaean era** started 3800 million years ago (m.y.a.), and the **Proterozoic era** (which had three periods) began 2500 m.y.a. Vertebrates, animals with backbones, were not observed until the **Paleozoic era** starting 544 m.y.a. and the only representative samples were fishes, amphibians, and early reptiles. The next **Mesozoic era** was when reptiles fully emerged, including dinosaurs as well as primitive birds. It began 245 m.y.a., had three periods (the Triassic, the Jurassic, and the Cretaceous), and ended with significant extinction of plant and animal life, including dinosaurs. The **Cenozoic or recent life period** (discussed on another card) began 65 m.y.a. Different plant life emerged during these periods as well.

Cenozoic Era

The Cenozoic era is the most recent. It began 65 million years ago with the **tertiary period**, which is divided into five epochs. The oldest epoch, the *Paleocene*, produced the mammals. Beginning 54 m.y.a., the *Eocene* epoch was a period of warm tropical climates in which the modern orders of mammals and anthropoids emerged and primates similar to prosimians were prevalent. About 38 m.y.a., the *Oligocene* epoch began, characterized by cooler, dry weather in the north, anthropoids in Africa, and growing distinctions between the primates. In the *Miocene* epoch, beginning 23 m.y.a., the cool, dry climate area extended toward middle latitudes, and Africa and Eurasia collided. The *Pliocene* epoch, which started 5 m.y.a., is characterized by emergence of Australopithecine hominids and Ardipithecus. The **quaternary period** of the Cenozoic era is divided into the Pleistocene and Holocene epochs. The *Pleistocene* or ice age epoch began somewhere around 1.6 to 1.8 m.y.a. and was a period of climatic changeability and glaciation and also the time that the genus Homo appeared. The modern or Holocene epoch began 10,000 to 11,000 years ago when warmer temperatures began and agriculture became prevalent.

Early Primates

Tropical and subtropical climates prevailed during the early **Cenozoic era** providing vegetation. **Early primates** were driven by adjustment to arboreal life and a heightened sense of sight. While there is equivocal evidence that some early primates probably existed during the Paleocene epoch, fossil records definitely confirm early primates during the next Eocene epoch (~54 to 38 m.y.a.). A 55-million-year-old skull of a euprimate, a mammal with some primate characteristics like frontward eyes and a large braincase, was recently found in China and named *Teilhardina asiatica*. A wide variety of prosimians lived in what we now call North America, Europe, Asia, and Africa,

- 125 -

which were all interconnected or almost connected (Africa). At some point, certain prosimians began to develop characteristics associated with anthropoids, such as more diurnal behavior and larger brains and eyes. By the Oligocene epoch (~38-23 m.y.a.), anthropoids predominated. There is fossil evidence primarily from Egypt of probable ancestors to New World monkeys, the parapithecid family, as well as the later catarrhines, the propliopithecid family which shares dentition patterns.

Miocene Epoch Hominoids

During the Miocene epoch (~23-5 m.y.a.), early **hominoids** antecedent to but different from present-day apes evolved. Fossils from the early part of the epoch indicate three species of the *Proconsul* group in Africa, characterized by dentition similar to current apes but a skeleton more like that of a monkey. Approximately 16 m.y.a. at the start of the middle part of the **Miocene epoch**, a **land bridge** developed between Eurasia and Africa providing migratory opportunities. Fossils of protoapes from this time have been discovered in various areas usually coexisting with our genus of *Homo erectus*. These include the extremely large *Gigantopithecus*, which probably lived in Asia until about 400,000 years ago. More recent finds from this time period include *Pierolapithecus catalaunicus*, from about 13 m.y.a. in Spain, which some believe is the last common ancestor to modern great apes including humans; *Sahelanthropus tchadensis* or Toumai, from about 7 to 6 m.y.a. in Chad, possibly the oldest known human descendant; *Orrorin tugenensis*, from about 6 m.y.a in Kenya, a bipedal creature with many resemblances to a chimp; and *Ardipithecus* (discussed elsewhere).

Bipedalism

Bipedalism, the ability to walk upright on two feet, is considered the fundamental feature that distinguishes early hominins from apes. The earliest identified and recognized ones belong to the genus *Ardipithecus,* examples of which have been found in Ethiopia dating from 5.8 to 4.4 m.y.a. Most experts believe that bipedalism developed during the Miocene epoch in some primates because of geological factors more than 5 million years ago. There was a shift toward a cooler, drier climate and more grassland in Africa. There was also a sinking of the Rift Valley and development of mountains in what is present-day Ethiopia, Kenya, and Tanzania. Primates east of this range started using bipedalism in order to navigate the grasslands more easily and view predators, while still sleeping and hiding in trees. Another explanation is that walking upright kept these hominins cooler due to less exposure to solar radiation. To the west of this range, the environment had more trees and was more humid, favoring chimpanzees.

Traits Other Than Bipedalism That Characterize Hominins

Hominins are the tribe that humans belong to. Early hominins had much smaller brains, similar in size to those of a chimpanzee, than modern humans. **Brain size** relative to other parts of the anatomy has increased over the ages because of the demands of upright bipedal locomotion. The **pelvic and trunk regions** need to be smaller for posture. Walking upright makes it difficult to have too large of a pelvic opening. Brain and **skull size** also became larger because humans have an extended period of childhood dependency. Early hominins had larger back teeth than modern humans because they needed them to chew tough, fibrous vegetation in the grasslands. As humans evolved, **dentition** has gotten smaller. Early hominins created and used **tools**, which was facilitated by bipedalism. Use of tools is still unique to hominins.

Early Hominins Ardipithecus and Kenyanthropus

Along with several of the *Australopithecus* species, these are two of the **earliest known hominins**, or human line after its division from ancestral chimps. Currently, *Ardipithecus kadabba* is considered to be the oldest known hominin because it appears to have been **bipedal**. Fossils dating from 5.8 m.y.a. were found in Ethiopia. Other members called *Ardipithecus ramidus* dating to 4.4 m.y.a. were also discovered in Ethiopia. *Kenyanthropus platyops* was discovered in Kenya and is considered by some to be a different branch of the human family tree because it has a flatter face and smaller molars. It dates to 3.5 million years ago.

Earliest Australopithecines

Australopithecines are prehistoric primates resembling humans dating to the **Pliocene epoch**. Six known species have been placed into this genus. The earliest example is *Australopithecus anamensis* found at two different sites in Kenya dating from 4.2 and 3.9 m.y.a. *A. anamensis* may have developed from *Ardipithecus ramidus*. It was bipedal and had thick molars and large canines. The species generally thought to be a predecessor to all later species of this genus was *Australopithecus afarensis* ("Lucy" and others) with fossil finds in Tanzania and Ethiopia dating it to between 3.8 and 3 million years ago. Fossils indicate many apelike attributes including dentition patterns, a cranial size only a little larger than that of a chimpanzee, and marked sexual dimorphism. Both of these Australopithecines were bipedal, however, which is the major reason they are considered human ancestors. There is another species called *A. garhi* discovered in Africa dating from 2.6 to 1.2 m.y.a.

Differences in Dentition Between Chimpanzees, Humans, and *A. Afarensis*

Early Australopithecines such as *A. Afarensis* are considered to be **dividing points** between chimpanzees and humans because although they were bipedal, they still had some qualities more reminiscent of chimps. In particular, the dentition pattern of *A. afarensis* is still closer to that of a chimpanzee than a human, reflecting their diet of coarse, fibrous savanna vegetation. Humans have much smaller back molars than the others, less pronounced canines, no diastema or gap between incisors and canines, and a more rounded, parabolic arch. Chimpanzees and *Australopithecus afarensis* both have relatively large molars, prominent canines, and diastemas, although the canine of the chimpanzee is much larger and more pointed. Adults of all three have a 2.1.2.3 dentition pattern in each quadrant of two/2 incisors, one/1 canine, two/2 premolars, and 3/three molars.

Evidence That Australopithecines were Bipedal

Australopithecines had a shorter and broader pelvis than apes, and the sacrum, which anchors the side bones, was wide. Their thigh bone was at an angle to the hip instead of straight as with an ape. They had a lumbar or lower spinal curve. Fossil records show that the foramen magnum or hole connecting the spinal cord to the brain was further forward and more centrally located in the Australopithecines than chimpanzees. All of these things make it easier to **walk upright**. The pelvises of Australopithecines are similar to but not exactly like those found in the later *Homo* species.

Gracile and Robust Australopithecines

Three species of more recent and relatively **robust** Australopithecines were found in Africa. Various theories suggest they developed from *A. afarensis* and that the **gracile** form either came first or overlapped in time with the robust forms. In any event, the smaller, less robust, so-called gracile species is represented by the South African *A. Africanus* which is dated to approximately 3 to

2 million years ago. Examples of **hyper-robust** Australopithecines include *A. robustus* and *A. boisei*; they had big, strong bones, teeth, and muscles and were thus very robust. They have been dated to ~2 to 1 m.y.a. and 2.6 to 1.2 m.y.a. and were found in South and East Africa, respectively. Their dentition was slightly different than earlier Australopithecines in that the canines were smaller, premolars were bicuspid, and molars were larger. The hyper-robust examples developed a sagittal crest at the pinnacle of the skull due to chewing. On average, all three weighed more and had larger brain sizes than earlier species

Division into the Two Genera of *Australopithecus* and *Homo*

It is believed that the hominins split into the **two genera** of *Australopithecus* and *Homo* more than 2 million years ago. The primary reason was reproductive remoteness. There was a time period where both existed in Africa until about 1.2 million years ago. The first known example of the *Homo* genus was *Homo habilis*, which had smaller teeth than Australopithecines and has been dated to approximately 2.4 to 1.4 m.y.a. *Homo erectus* lived around 1.9 to 1.4 million years ago. It had a bigger brain with regions that could regulate higher mental functions. The splitting of the genera has been explained in a number of ways. Some think that the two split from *Australopithecus afarensis* while others think only other Australopithecines evolved from it and eventually became extinct.

Possible Role of Tool Making

The oldest discovered tools are **Oldowan stone pebble tools**, which were found originally in Tanzania and later in other African areas. They date back as far as about 2.5 to 2 million years ago. There are two basic types: **cores**, used mainly for pounding, and **flakes**, utilized for cutting or scraping. Most experts have long believed that these tools were made by *Homo habilis*. However, there is some more recent evidence that at least one species of *Australopithecus, A. garhi*, also used stone tools around 2.5 million years ago in the area now called Ethiopia because these types of tools were found near the aforementioned fossils.

Homo Rudolfensis

Homo rudolfensis is a fossil discovered in Kenya, also known as **KNM-ER 1470**. It shows both a very large brain, indicative of *Homo* species, and also extremely big molars, suggestive of *Australopithecus* species. It has been variously dated to anywhere from 2.4 to 1.8 million years ago. The main reason it was assigned to the *Homo* genus was the large brain size. Some paleoanthropologists believe it is an example of *Homo habilis*, perhaps male, while others see differences between the two. The KNM-ER 1470 skull is larger than a typical *H. habilis* skull, does not have as striking a brow ridge, and has a longer and flatter face.

Relationship Between *Homo Habilis* and *Homo Erectus*

The Leakeys first discovered fossils of *Homo habilis* in Tanzania in 1960 and felt that it was a predecessor to *Homo erectus*. However, very recent fossil findings in Kenya suggest that the time frames for the two intersected and that sexual dimorphism existed in both. *Homo habilis* is now dated from 1.9 to 1.44 million years ago, and *Homo erectus* (earliest known called *H. ergaster*) is dated from 1.9 to 1 million years ago. Both species resided in close proximity for about a half million years. The *H. erectus* depended more on hunting and developed more specialized tools, however, and therefore show different dentition such as smaller back teeth.

Adaptive Traits of *Homo Erectus*

Homo erectus had a skeleton that was rough but surprisingly similar to modern humans, and they had longer legs than prior hominins. These traits facilitated **hunting**. They had a cranium about twice as large as the Australopithecines and close in size to *Homo sapiens*, but *H. erectus* had thicker skull bones, a wider and flatter shaped skull, and larger teeth, face, and jaws. All of these features were adaptations that facilitated hunting. They had learned about **fire** which made it possible for them to exist in caves, cook, and migrate to cooler climates. Fossils assigned to *Homo erectus* have been found as far from Africa as Dmanisi in Georgia (former Soviet Republic), Java, Italy, and several places in China. *Homo erectus* also made fairly complicated tools (discussed elsewhere). It cannot be proven whether or not they had a spoken language but the arrangement of their **vocal apparatus** was very similar to modern humans.

Pleistocene Epoch and the Evolution of Archaic Forms of *Homo Sapiens*

The Pleistocene epoch began about 1.8 million years ago. Towards the end of its **Lower period** around one million years ago, a number of ice ages or **glacials** interspersed with warmer periods called **interglacials**. During glacials, continental ice sheets pressed forward in North America and Europe and cooled the climate, and during interglacials they drew back. *Homo sapiens* lived during the latter part of the Middle and all of the Latter Pleistocene subdivisions. Early or archaic forms of *Homo sapiens* have been found in Europe, Africa, and Asia dating from about 300,000 to 28,000 years ago. They are separated into those who are believed to be ancestors of modern man and the Neanderthals. Teams have also discovered slightly earlier fossils that may be transitional (*H. heidelbergensis* in Germany) or a possible link between Neanderthals and anatomically modern humans (*H. antecessor* in Spain).

Neanderthals

The Neanderthals or *Homo sapiens neanderthalensis* are a group of archaic *H. sapiens* hunters. They primarily occupied Europe and the Middle East approximately 130,000 to 28,000 years ago, although examples have been found as distant as Siberia. **Neanderthal** fossils were discovered as long ago as 1856 in the **German Neander Valley**. Neanderthals display features that illustrate their adaptation to extremely cold glacial periods. They were relatively short and hefty with large trunks in comparison to their arms and legs. They had substantial nasal passages and long, wide noses. Their front teeth were massive, suggesting they may have used them for purposes other than just mastication, such as preparing hides to make clothing. Their facial features were wide and their brow ridges were sizeable. Later Neanderthal examples from the Wurm glacial time period starting around 75,000 years ago have less pronounced front teeth and brow ridges. This is presumably due to development of more sophisticated tools in the so-called **Mousterian tradition**. Neanderthals were the first hominids to bury their dead.

Relationship Between Neanderthals and Anatomically Modern Humans

It is currently held that Neanderthals were simply supplanted in Europe by **anatomically modern humans (AMHs)**. Experts feel that *Homo erectus* separated into two groups that evolved eventually into Neanderthals and AMHs. The average brain size of Neanderthals was smaller than AMHs, 1430 versus 1350 cubic centimeters. Most fossil records indicate differently shaped brain cases and other facial features. AMHs had more rounded and higher brain cases, a more prominent forehead, more distinct chins, less heavy brows, and less massive front teeth. It is felt that anatomically modern humans such as Cro-Magnon, Skhul, Qafzeh, and Herto began in Africa and then migrated into Europe and Asia, displacing the Neanderthals and perhaps also interbreeding with them. Some call this the "out of Africa theory" or **Recent African Origin model**.

DNA Evidence Supporting Differences

A 1997 study comparing DNA from a Neanderthal's upper arm bone to that of a modern reference DNA sample indicated twenty-seven **discrepancies** as opposed to a maximum of eight **divergences** from different modern populations. More recent sequencing of nuclear and mitochondrial DNA (mtDNA) from another Neanderthal fossil indicates that the Neanderthal had a significantly dissimilar Y or male chromosome from modern humans, suggesting little procreation between the Neanderthals and anatomically modern humans (AMHs). An older study in 1987 examined mtDNA in women with ancestors from various areas. Mitochondrial DNA, which is extracted from the cytoplasm of cells, was selected because it is contributed only by the mother in the fertilized ovum. This investigation showed a great deal of variation in those of African descent. Using a technique called **molecular dating**, which assumes a certain mutation rate, it concluded that modern humans are descended from a woman living about 200,000 years ago ("Eve").

Theory of Multiregional Evolution

Multiregional evolution (MRE) is the theory that *Homo sapiens* evolved from *Homo erectus* in all areas occupied by humans. This is opposed to the **out of Africa theory**, which purports that the origin was only in Africa followed by movement to Europe and elsewhere (discussed further on other cards). The **multiregional evolution theory** was mainly put forth in the late 1990s by **Milford Wolpoff**, who contends that there has always been interbreeding and gene flow and that any type of selective improvement would be disseminated. He and his followers believe that the evolution from *H. erectus* to *H. sapiens* occurred regionally. This theory is supported by observations that distinctive regional features found today are evident in *Homo erectus* fossils found in the same area. According to multiregional evolution, if there was a common ancestor or "Eve," she existed far before the timeframe suggested by the out of Africa theory.

Homo Floresiensis

Homo floresiensis is a newly identified *Homo* species found on the Indonesian island of **Flores**. These fossils, dated from about 95,000 to as recently as 13,000 years ago, show miniature archaic humans derived from *Homo erectus*. They show extremely small skulls, approximately 370 cubic centimeters. It is believed that isolation on the island coupled with atypical evolutionary forces caused all animals there to exhibit either gigantism or dwarfism. *H. floresiensis* apparently made quite complex tools, used fire, and perhaps had some type of language. There was a volcano about 12,000 years ago in the region where these were discovered which obliterated them.

Disciplines That Often Work Together with Physical Anthropologists

Physical anthropologists often work in partnership with archeologists or other scientists. Whereas **physical anthropologists** glean information through looking at fossil records, **archeologists** examine artifacts. Complementary disciplines include **paleontology**, the examination of ancient life through fossil records, and **palynology**, the analysis of ancient plants and ecosystems utilizing pollen samples. For example, plant crystals or phytoliths are often found on teeth or artifacts. Other types of scientists that may work in conjunction with physical anthropologists and archeologists are geologists, geographers, physicists, and chemists. The relatively new and high-tech procedure of **remote sensing** is increasingly being employed. Remote sensing is the utilization of satellite imaging and aerial photography to detect potentially valuable ground sites.

Use of Bone Biology in Physical Anthropology

Bone or **skeletal biology** is the examination of bone as a biological tissue. It is fundamental to the work of **physical anthropologists**. Bone can be studied from many different perspectives, such as its genetics, biomechanics, osteology, or paleopathology. **Biomechanics** refers to the way in which movement is constructed, osteology is the examination of skeletal differences and their causes, and paleopathology looks at the way in which disease or injury affected skeletal remains. **Forensic anthropology** generally uses bone biology to look at more recent human remains in order to figure out a cause of death and other characteristics. An overall term for body measurement research is **anthropometry**.

Stratigraphy and Relative Dating of Remains

Fossils, artifacts, and other material remains can be dated either by relative or absolute (chronometric) dating. **Relative dating** is facilitated by **stratigraphy**, the examination of how the earth sediments into discrete layers or strata. The **law of superposition** states that unless a disturbance has occurred, new layers are superimposed over older ones and stratigraphy can be used to establish a relative chronological sequence. Relative dating ascertains a time frame for a particular remain based on the strata it is found in and relative to remains of other plants and animals that presumably lived at the same time. It does not give a definitive date. Older remains are found in deeper strata and vice versa. Relative dating also uses fluorine absorption analysis, which utilizes the principle that bones from the same period take in similar percentages of fluorine.

Radiocarbon Dating for Absolute Dating of Remains

Absolute dating of remains is more precise dating through more scientific techniques than relative dating. Each radiometric technique quantifies **radioactive decay**. Organic materials up to 40,000 years old are dated using ^{14}C, the radioactive isotope of carbon (stable version ^{12}C) which is absorbed in plants from cosmic radiation and later in animals that eat these plants or other animals. The time of death or vestiges from a fire can be dated using the carbon-14 half-life of 5730 years, when half of the isotope is converted into stable nitrogen (^{14}N). Small samples can now be dated using **accelerator mass spectrometry (AMS)** which actually counts the number of carbon-14 atoms.

Non-Carbon-Based Radiometric Dating Techniques for Absolute Dating of Remains

Very old materials from a half-million years ago or more can be dated by looking at the conversion of the much longer half-life radioisotope of **potassium ^{40}K** into the gas **argon-40** (potassium/argon or K/Ar dating). This method is used to date inorganic rocks and minerals (primarily volcanic rock) by heating the rock to allow the release of trapped argon gas. A more accurate modification of this technique is argon/argon or Ar/Ar dating which calculates the decay of one argon isotope into another (^{40}Ar to ^{39}Ar). **Uranium series dating** uses fission tracks from decay of the uranium isotope ^{238}U into lead, ^{234}U into thorium, or other uranium isotopes to date materials anywhere from 1000 to 1 million years old. Similar time periods for rocks and minerals can also be established using **thermoluminescence**, which quantifies the energy captured from radioactive decay in nearby soil, or **electron spin resonance (ESR)**, which measures the accumulation of electrons on crystalline materials.

Dendrochronology for Absolute Dating of Remains

Dendrochronology or **tree-ring dating** is used for absolute dating of wood or charcoal materials up to about 11,000 years old. Tree growth is indicated by a new ring every year. Climatic variations

- 131 -

affect the ring pattern, which should be similar in all area trees from the same time period. For example, wide rings indicate wetter years, while narrow ones point to dry years. Ring patterns on trees can be crossdated or matched by observation and statistical analysis, and this crossdating can also be used to pinpoint dates for wood or charcoal samples from ancient buildings or other artifacts. The technique can only be used with tree species that thrive in climates with distinct seasons such as juniper, oak, and pine.

Methods of Dating Remains Beyond Stratigraphy and Absolute Dating Techniques

Any dating method based on comparing cultural shifts is considered a **cultural technique**. One legitimate example is **seriation** or the recognition that there is a regular substitution of one artifact style for another. **Paleomagnetism**, which can only be used to date materials with magnetic minerals from about the last 2000 years, is another technique based on the movement of the earth's magnetic poles and their documented positions. **Obsidian hydration** is a method that can be used to date volcanic glass up to 800,000 years old. It is founded on the principle that obsidian glass forms a hydration layer over time as it reacts with water. Bones can be dated utilizing **amino acid racemization** or a shift in polarity of aspartic acid.

Thank You

We at Mometrix would like to extend our heartfelt thanks to you, our friend and patron, for allowing us to play a part in your journey. It is a privilege to serve people from all walks of life who are unified in their commitment to building the best future they can for themselves.

The preparation you devote to these important testing milestones may be the most valuable educational opportunity you have for making a real difference in your life. We encourage you to put your heart into it—that feeling of succeeding, overcoming, and yes, conquering will be well worth the hours you've invested.

We want to hear your story, your struggles and your successes, and if you see any opportunities for us to improve our materials so we can help others even more effectively in the future, please share that with us as well. **The team at Mometrix would be absolutely thrilled to hear from you!** So please, send us an email (support@mometrix.com) and let's stay in touch.

If you'd like some additional help, check out these other resources we offer for your exam:

http://MometrixFlashcards.com/GACE

Additional Bonus Material

Due to our efforts to try to keep this book to a manageable length, we've created a link that will give you access to all of your additional bonus material.

Please visit http://www.mometrix.com/bonus948/gacebehavsci to access the information.